Ionized

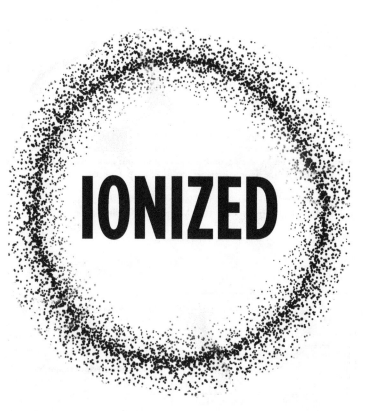

IONIZED

Construct a Self-Sustaining Office and
Build an Empowering Positive Environment
That Breeds Long-Term Success

MATT WILLS

NEW YORK

LONDON • NASHVILLE • MELBOURNE • VANCOUVER

IONIZED

Construct a Self-Sustaining Office and Build an Empowering Positive Environment That Breeds Long-Term Success

Published in New York, New York, by Morgan James Publishing. Morgan James is a trademark of Morgan James, LLC. www.MorganJamesPublishing.com

Proudly distributed by Ingram Publisher Services.

Morgan James BOGO™

A **FREE** ebook edition is available for you or a friend with the purchase of this print book.

_____

CLEARLY SIGN YOUR NAME ABOVE

Instructions to claim your free ebook edition:
1. Visit MorganJamesBOGO.com
2. Sign your name CLEARLY in the space above
3. Complete the form and submit a photo of this entire page
4. You or your friend can download the ebook to your preferred device

ISBN 9781631957093 paperback
ISBN 9781631957109 ebook
Library of Congress Control Number: 2021942380

Cover and Interior Design by:
Chris Treccani
www.3dogcreative.net

Morgan James PUBLISHING Builds with... **Habitat for Humanity** Peninsula and Greater Williamsburg

Morgan James is a proud partner of Habitat for Humanity Peninsula and Greater Williamsburg. Partners in building since 2006.

Get involved today! Visit MorganJamesPublishing.com/giving-back

Ionized [ahy-uhn-ahyz]
Verb
To convert an individual or group by adding a positive charge, often in conjunction with self-improvement and success. The result of the charged individuals is called an ION.

Table of Contents

Acknowledgments

Writing a book isn't always going to be as difficult as it sounds. In my opinion, the hardest part of writing a book is simply sitting down and getting started. That process wouldn't have begun as soon or ended as quickly if it wasn't for the leadership of Matt Smithson and Asia Ellmer. Matt has played a key role in guiding my career and the moment I brought up the idea to write a book, he was behind me 100 percent of the way! From the moment I began working with Asia, she has challenged me every step of the way. Whether it's the method in which I work or changing my perspective, Asia constantly forces me to evolve as a person.

To my wife, Altagracia, and my daughter, Michelle, thank you for all the love and distraction you give. If the two of you weren't in my life, I wouldn't have the aspirations that I have. This journey takes the three of us, and I think about that every day.

To my mom, Michele, thank you for your undying belief in me. I'm incredibly lucky to have the sounding board and support I have in you.

To Justin Bedsole, thanks for being the perfect co-manager. I appreciate you holding down the fort while I took extra time to write this. Also, again, thanks for being a great sounding board.

To Andy Marlowe, Chad Martin, and Tom Dettloff, thank you for providing me the best opportunity to learn and grow within the industry. I am incredibly grateful for the work that I have.

To the Morgan James Publishing family, thank you for seeing value in my work and showing me constant positivity through the process. This experience has been incredible.

Thank you Aubrey Kosa for editing my work. It's always good to have a professional, outside perspective take a look and make it more streamlined. Thanks for the awesome work you do.

Introduction

My name is Matt Wills, and I work in the ever-illustrious, door-to-door industry managing a canvassing department for an office of a solar installation company called ION Solar.

Being relatively new to the industry, I have thus far maintained an "outside looking in" understanding of how the door-to-door industry works. Having a different—and fresh—perspective moving into a management role in a new industry had me picking apart processes and metrics to understand the current industry standards. Upon working through all the details with a magnifying glass and a fine-toothed comb, I have come to the conclusion that the door-to-door industry standards are inherently flawed and currently vestigial. I felt compelled to write this book and provide more comprehensive alternatives to many of the processes as well as the metrics used to show productivity.

Working in the door-to-door industry has definitely been an adventure that has brought out both the worst and the best in me. It's an industry that has challenged me every step of the way. Due to my growth within and understanding of ION Solar, I have been fortunate enough to play a large part in building out office structures for various levels and departments to promote growth and productivity.

This book is written as a how-to guide from beginning to end, demonstrating the methods, policies, systems, and structures we have constructed to enable a highly productive office running sustainably at its current capacity. The best part is that we are not even close to reaching our potential.

In fact, in my opinion, it's best to always think that you will never reach your limitations.

In this book, I start at the beginning and take you through the turmoil of starting at the bottom of a company, working through various situations, entering a managerial position, and challenging the status quo with comprehensive alterations to the office environment. Along the way, I point out systemic flaws which we address and correct later on. I also point out my own lack of understanding and trace the development of my perspective over time. We break down the psychological aspects of policies and their and expand upon the procedures I use to determine the value of standard office policies, as well as any issues that are provoked by those policies. In addition, we break down statistics and data from old systems to new systems while showing the direction, progression, and evolution involved in creating an environment that empowers its people.

Of course, we also go over the mechanics and theory of management as they apply to an office environment. I provide a road map for learning from statistics as well as developing culture and leadership. I also share a step-by-step guide for a system of policies that will allow you to stand back and watch your office produce on its own.

I appreciate you picking up this book. As they say, leaders are readers. I believe reading is easily the quickest way to fast-track our understanding and perspectives, and I am honored to be part of your rotation.

Chapter 1:

COVID and Camaraderie

February 2020, Virginia Beach, VA—I join a door-to-door solar sales company, ION Solar. ION Solar's sales department is divided into three tiers: setters, self-gen, and closers.

The setters are door-to-door canvassers whose jobs are simply to schedule appointments for the company. They do not sell. They do not answer questions or give any detailed information. They just recite a pitch designed to pique homeowners' interest just enough to be willing to sit with a "specialist" (closer) for "forty-five minutes" (two hours).

Once a setter has become proficient and consistent in their role, they can move into what is called the self-gen role. This means that an individual now has the ability to close their own deals, but they are only allowed to sell to homeowners they found through knocking on doors.

Finally, once a self-gen becomes skilled at closing their own deals, they can then become closers. Closers have the privilege of taking leads from the company, though they are encouraged to knock on doors as well.

This three-tiered system allows the office to run like a well-oiled machine—if implemented correctly. It also allows employees to see the opportunity along the way.

A common promise that you hear in most sales organizations is: "You get out what you put in." In other words, the harder you work, the more successful you become. The more you grind, the more money you make. The more proficient you are at your job, the quicker you can move up. The funny thing is that in most companies I've worked for, that idea is not full-fledged. Often salespeople must first fight through an obstacle course of tenure, nepotism, and just really who management likes as a friend or person. In someone's current position, "you get out what you put in" is usually correct; however, to move up the ladder is generally more of a political game than a work game.

Personally, I have an extensive sales background. Prior to working for ION Solar, I worked for an exterior remodeling company but left due to poor business practices. I was looking for a company where I could thrive as a salesman, and my search didn't go exactly how I thought ... It turned out ION Solar has a rite of passage. Everyone has to start as a setter regardless of their background. This, of course, is a buffer to keep out the giant egos. If someone is too good to knock on doors, they don't belong here. Still, the last thing I wanted to do was knock on doors. Actually, I had never knocked on doors. I thought that type of work was below me. In fact, I had no respect for people who knocked on doors or even the people who managed those departments.

Clearly, this wasn't a productive thought process, but everyone is a work in progress.

The only reason I decided to give the job a shot was because I knew how much money some of these guys were making. Legends from the exterior remodeling industry who were consistently earning over $150,000 per year were leaving their stable jobs to come knock on doors for ION. It wasn't something I planned to look back on with regret. Besides, I thought, how hard could knocking on doors be? If there's anything I have, it's work ethic. If they only expect six hours of work a day here, I'm going to give them ten a day to show them I'm serious.

Day 1—I get out early on a Saturday. I'm fired up to get started and blow past the first stage. I picked out a neighborhood, planned my route, psyched myself up, drove there, and got out of my car. All of the sudden, I'm on the street looking at strangers' houses, and all I can think about is that I'm the intruder who's about to knock. That's an uncomfortable feeling. All sales I had previously made had been warm and expected. No one was going to want me knocking on their door. It was crazy. My high faded quickly, and I had these homes staring me in the face. It's funny how quickly your perspective can change when you're thrown into a situation. Something that seemed to be the simplest job in the world had just become the most uncomfortable feeling I ever had. Of course, I needed to fight through it. I was visibly nervous for the first door I knocked on, even a little shaky. The door opened, the person who answered asked why I was there, and I began to fumble through a pitch that I didn't even have completely memorized. While I spoke, I was hardly coherent and fairly red with embarrassment. Why was this so difficult for me?! I had never had an issue speaking in front of groups or explaining a thesis but bothering a person in their own home was a new experience that

I didn't much care for. That person let me know they rented the home, so it was on to the next.

I continued knocking for five straight hours.

I was actually moving at a decent pace, changing up my pitch, trying new things. Of course, I was stumbling through every bit of it, and the rejection was wearing me down fast. I walked past many "no soliciting" signs. If there were too many cars in a driveway, I'd feel overwhelmed, and when it started getting dark, I called it a night. By the end of my first day, I had generated a total of zero leads. I was completely disheartened and decided to take Sunday to think about what I could have done differently or better and get back at it on Monday.

The Virginia Beach office has meetings every Monday and Thursday. This office was much smaller than any other sales office I had been a part of, which made me doubt the company. The office was on the second floor of an office building and consisted of an entry room, a tiny box of a meeting area, a personal office with a small desk, and a kitchen/hallway that led to a really small room where merch was stored. I can't imagine the office was more than 500 square feet.

At the time, there were about fifteen setters and eight salesmen—a fairly small operation. However, that didn't seem to take away from this office as they had been the number-one office in the company four months in a row! These were highly productive people.

Over those last four months, the office had been working toward a unified goal: "Beat Vegas!" The Las Vegas office was a powerhouse forever neck and neck with Virginia Beach, and Virginia Beach had been continuously edging them out.

This office had four managers, which is unusual considering its size. There were two setter managers, Justin and Asia, as well as two closer managers, Tom and Chad.

Justin is a bear of a guy, a bearded ocean fisherman with a heart of gold. Justin's managerial style, however, was strict and based on fear. He liked to run a tight ship. The upper management of ION didn't approve of this style of managing, so his hands—and ideas—were tied and took a backseat to Asia.

Asia, on the other hand, is a fit, attractive blonde girl typically rocking overly revealing skintight leggings. Her online handle is "Solar Barbie." She's not usually the type of person you'd see knocking on doors. Asia constantly works on her managerial skills in all areas. She has something to prove, and no one is going to outwork Asia. Her managerial style is the opposite of Justin's—compassionate to a fault.

Tom is a tall, handsome ex-marine. He's rigid, no-nonsense, and by the book. He has the right way of doing everything, so he takes charge. "Consistency is King" is his motto, and his training and meetings reflect that as simple repetitions of the basics. He recruited most of the heavy hitters. This is Tom's office. Sure, Chad outranks him, but Tom is the man.

Chad is interesting, to say the least. Yet another physically fit manager in the office, he has dark hair, dark eyes, and a reputation for having a cold, robotic persona. The ironic thing is that he actually has very high emotional intelligence (EQ). He reveals minimal emotion; however, he still makes emotional decisions, which makes him a very difficult person to understand. Chad is great at being stoic. You can sit down across from him ready to tell him off and he will just listen. He'll look at you and say nothing. This will generally prompt you to continue talking until you've worked everything out in your mind without him ever saying a word. It's freakin' voodoo.

I pleaded with Chad quite often to allow me to skip the setter phase and get right to the self-gen phase. I wanted to show him the value I could bring to the team as a high-level closer. Of course, he wasn't going to let that happen. Instead, he helped me work on my pitch to fit my personality better.

For the next four weeks, I continued to knock on doors. I was miserable. I was a god-awful setter. I worked fifty-plus hours a week and generally had about six leads and maybe one of those would sit. I had to psyche myself into knocking nearly every time I walked up to a door.

In those early days, my main problem was that I was projecting. Projecting is a form of internal resistance. This is an issue common with people who are constantly in their own heads and tend to overthink things. It's a problem entirely between the ears. The idea that someone is going to be upset because you rang their doorbell is just that—an idea. It's the lens I chose to see the world through, even if it was incorrect. I was defeating myself and the possibility of success before even ringing the doorbell. It was a self-fulfilling prophecy. I had no idea who was inside the home. I had no idea if they were going to be upset or greet me kindly. I had no idea if solar was something they might be interested in. Honestly, they might not know it themselves. Every single "no soliciting" sign I passed, every time I walked by a house because the homeowner was outside working in their yard, every time I called it early because it was getting dark, I was projecting a false idea that spun me away from success. Every door is an opportunity, and I was keeping them all closed.

At one point, the company had everyone read a book called *Who Moved My Cheese?*. The book is a short story about two small, humanlike creatures and two rats who inhabit a maze in search of cheese. Long story short, while the humans were intellectually superior to the rats, they were prone to complacency and afraid of change. The rats, on the other hand, were prosperous in their adaptability and persistence to find success behind every corridor. This book got a rise out of me because it devalued the intelligence I believed to be far superior than that of a rat. Of course, stirring that emotion was the exact point of the book.

> Productivity is the name of the game, and intellect holds no value without execution.

Intellect doesn't pay; being productive does. Actions, more frequently and in greater quantity, will get you paid. Intellect is a tool and can help you or hurt you depending on your mindset. Intellect requires execution to manifest your ideas into something tangible and real.

There are people who might have the greatest story in the world floating around in their heads, but they've never sat down to write it. Some might have the greatest hit song to ever top the charts, but they never sat down to compose it. You may have the best new idea for a phone application that would be a massive hit and make you rich, but you never worked on it. And it won't be long before someone else has the same idea and makes it a reality. That's what happens to intellect without execution.

Recently, I sat down for a poker game with some friends and coworkers. This was not a subtle group of people. It was not exactly the group you'd find at a professional poker tournament, myself included. However, a couple of players were more advanced than the rest of us. This group had a tendency of going all in just about every other hand and then buying back in the next. It turned out to be a very reckless game of poker; however, it really made me think about the value of each hand. Because the stakes were always so high, you have to remember that most of the time, no one really has anything good. Therefore, if you have something good, you might as well play through. At the end of nearly every round that ended with a few players going all in, a few folded beforehand. But when all the cards were on the table, every single time there was one player who had folded shaking their head and showing everyone the hand that would have won the massive pot. "Look what I had!" they would object. And every time, you would hear another player singing a quick melody, "No one cares what you folded."

I found that line to be transcendent of the poker game, but let's think about it in poker terms. Say you have two of the same suit in your hand at the start of the round. They may not be high cards, but they are mid-level. Not a bad start. That's something to invest in or bet on. Then you get to see how that hand fairs compared to the flop. Say two of the three cards are of the same suit you are holding. Now things are looking good. So good, in fact, that you want to greatly increase your investment in what you hold in your hand. It turns out that other people have the same idea and start matching or increasing what you're willing to invest. Now intellect is going to get to you.

Do they have two cards of the same suit? Are their cards higher than your cards? Why would anyone risk so much on one decent hand? Am I making the right choice? Am I going to look stupid in front of my peers?

More often than not, these thoughts will get someone to give up on what they have. Now all the money they've invested getting to that point is lost because they were too afraid to follow through.

How is that any different from a dream or goal in the real world?

For example, when someone says, "I could've been a great actor. When I was young, everyone said I could've been in movies." Great! You may have been born with a natural talent but how much time did you invest in that talent? That talent is your pocket aces but how much money did you invest in the coaching and training of that talent? How much rejection did you go through before you had your first breakthrough that would finally get you noticed? How much did you invest in yourself before you gave up and settled for something safe and comfortable?

"No one cares what you folded."

That life could've existed, but it never had a chance. The truth is that everyone has the opportunity to be great, but not many take the time necessary to execute, and that intellect will eventually waste away as a far-fetched childhood dream. The moment you realize that something you have is good, take the time to follow through. You will soon realize things are not as far-fetched as you imagined. Those who experience success from following through will turn into naturally productive people as they continue benefiting from execution.

During the last week of February, the Virginia Beach office was once again neck and neck with Las Vegas. Actually, Las Vegas had a pretty solid lead going into that last week, and we had some ground to make up if we wanted to stay number one in the company. The office culture was very powerful during this time as we gathered around the same passion and competition that had possessed management. We were constantly saying and posting, "Beat Vegas!" The setter team and closer team were simultaneously hitting daily goals in order to pull ahead. On the very last day of the month, we were still behind, but we rallied and pulled off one of the strongest days of sales the company had ever seen. We had sales coming in all day, and Virginia Beach once again finished in first place!

While that was exciting, I couldn't afford to be a setter long enough to get good at it. I have a high overhead at home, and it just wasn't paying the bills. Knowing that I had been out working constantly, Chad decided to give me a pass. Now this was against office protocol. Normally a setter would have to consistently produce eight held appointments per week before they could move up, so this would be an experiment for the office. This is not necessarily a good practice for management considering that special treatment can make other workers bitter, but of course, I was looking out for myself and was very grateful. Luckily I know my skills as a salesman, and I had four sales in my first week as a self-gen. That turned some heads since no one really knew who I was.

My first week of sales was in mid-March of 2020. Since February, we had been hearing political rumblings of an overseas virus that was spreading fast, but like most people, we didn't quite understand the severity of what was about to happen. Every day, the threat loomed greater. Italy and other European countries began going through a crisis. Countries began locking down their travel, then their streets. Suddenly the world was in a pandemic. Before we knew it, COVID-19 was affecting all industries; many companies and small businesses were going under. Whether or not it was related to the pandemic, it seemed Las Vegas was no longer putting up competitive numbers. They seemed to be sliding down the leaderboard, which was completely unusual for them.

As luck would have it, because our business dealt with energy production, we were categorized as an "essential business." This categorization made it legal for us to continue operating without repercussion. Unfortunately, most of the setter team didn't want to continue to knock on doors and our production plummeted. I, however, never missed a day of work. My wife was locked out of country, and I was going to spend every waking moment working to earn the closer position.

While you might think I'm crazy for knocking on people's doors during a pandemic, you must know that I have a killer immune system and was not in a high-risk category. You may also think I'm crazy because homeowners would be furious. The truth was, I rarely ran into a person who was upset. In fact, because almost everyone was stuck working from home in those early months, nearly every homeowner I interacted with was stir-crazy. They just wanted to hang out with someone. Some days I'd knock on only five doors because I spent one to two hours hanging out with each homeowner. Rather than taking up too much time, this was also beneficial to me. The more someone likes you, the more willing they are to sit down and let you pitch them.

The aspect of the early pandemic days that was miserable is that the office as a whole wasn't productive. The setter side had fallen off, and the closers didn't want to knock on doors either. We also didn't have the ability to use our office to hold meetings anymore, so every meeting was held using videoconferencing. Out of desperation, management decided to hold meetings every single day as a way to fire everyone up and/or tell them that they needed to work. This just ended up taking time out of everyone's day and had the opposite of the desired effect. No one enjoyed this form of micromanagement, and everything the managers said slowly became white noise.

One day in the midst of this season, Asia called me up. She began venting about the setter team not producing despite the constant meetings. She needed to find a solution. "What can I do to get the setter team motivated?" she asked.

Now I'm not entirely sure if she was actually asking for my advice or just looking for a sounding board, but I've always been one to give my perspective. "You can't," I responded, which sounds like a harsh answer but there is a reason for it. "Every single day the management holds a meeting to motivate the team, this overbearance has turned what you say into white noise. What the setter team needs isn't management; it's camaraderie." I went on to explain that if she had the few setters who were currently active on the doors reach out and invite other setters, we would have a much better chance of production.

Asia, being Asia, didn't waste any time. She and Justin built an office structure that included what they called "team leads." The new team lead position in our office was given to four setters who were continuously working. The management divided the rest of the setters between the four team leads, who were supposed to invite and motivate the other setters. This sub-management position gave the few productive setters a sense of status and a slight pay increase.

Never underestimate the value of status. Status is a means for differentiating someone who excels. If you implement a status system correctly, you won't even need to pay more for each status. Workers will work hard for the reward of simply having status. I cover this in more depth later in the book.

Feeling better about the job after a few successful sales, I continued in my self-gen position. In the month of April, I sold six accounts. While this number is low, the closer team's average was seven, so I couldn't (and didn't) feel too bad about it. I reached out to both Chad and Tom about possibly moving up to the closer role, but both of them gave me vague answers like "you need to be more productive" or "volumes speak volumes." I was not happy about these answers. I needed a metric to aim for. Give me a number, and I will put my all into achieving that number. "More productive" could mean a variety of things, and I needed a clear expectation.

By the end of April, two other offices had jumped ahead of our production. Both were in the state of Utah, and the powerhouse was now Salt Lake City. Salt Lake City had a commanding lead over even the next-highest-producing office. We had some work to do.

May came along, and I was off to my best month yet! I knew I was an asset to this team, but it was impossible to get that recognition out of Tom. I was out constantly, taking new setters and self-gen with me, trying my best to be a team player while still being productive. What bothered me is that while I was doing twice as much work as a closer, the office still refused to send me a lead. It was something I brought up quite a few times, and the management wasn't happy that I asked for it. The more I asked, the less chance I had. Of course, I knew that I wasn't entitled to leads at the self-gen position, but without a clear expectation of the number I needed to hit to become a closer, I was constantly confused and working without direction. This, of course, made me upset. I couldn't make sense of anything.

By the end of May, I had sold eight accounts. The closer team averaged nine, so I was exactly where I was the month before. One day while I was knocking on doors, I answered a call from Chad who told me that I needed to be more productive. This was incredibly upsetting for me because, again, I had to find my own appointments and was doing twice the work of a closer. And I was keeping up with the closers! Logically, this made no sense to me and frustrated me to my core. "If you want me to be more productive, give me some leads," I said.

That was the wrong answer.

After that, Chad stopped all communication with me. It was like I had burned a bridge. I wasn't sure how I was going to become a closer or possibly a manager after that. If I really wanted to make it work at this company, the only choice I had was to keep my head down and produce at a much higher volume.

By the end of May, Virginia Beach had slid down to fourth place in the company, which I'm sure was not a comfortable feeling for the management. Another new office had taken the lead. The king was Denver this time. At one point, Virginia Beach had been known as the office with the target on their back but now that seemed to be getting away from us. That didn't stop the management from constructing a bigger vision. The new motto was: "Road to 200!" Denver had produced over 140 sales, but no office had seen anything like 200. If you set your goal higher than the offices ahead of you, there's a good chance you will pass them up!

June came around, and people started coming back to work. Recruitment was happening fast, and things seem to be getting back on track. As a way for me to help the setter organization a little bit, I declared that for every account I sold, I was going to add a setter to the account. This was not something that people did. As a self-gen, I was paid more per account than the closers because I had to find the customers to work with. However, adding a setter to the account meant that the company would reduce my extra pay and give it to the setter instead. My policy was that I would add the setters I saw out grinding on the doors, and it worked as a motivator.

In the first two weeks of June, I had sold six accounts. This was shaping up to be my best month yet. Also, every day, I got out with new setters to help develop them as well. The setter management team was thrilled with me. The closer manager team, however, was indifferent.

One day, Tom decided to shadow one of my appointments. Unfortunately, even though I'm a good salesman, whenever I have management with me, I get super nervous and revert to the industry sales techniques that I normally wouldn't use. I always feel like I have to do all the "by the book" techniques to showcase them for my boss, and that makes the experience for the homeowner a bit awkward. I did manage to get this particular lady to go for it when Tom shadowed me, but unfortunately she was turned down for poor credit.

After the appointment, I sat down with Tom so that he could give me some critiques. He didn't approve of some of my methods, and we went back and forth on the different selling styles. After we had gone over it for about fifteen minutes, Tom looked at me and said, "You need to be more productive, man!"

Oh man did this get to me. Every single month, I had been 50 percent more productive than the last, and I was keeping up with the closers. I looked at Tom, confused, and replied, "I'm keeping up with the closers!"

He pulled out the stats to show me that while most of the closers had seven or eight accounts, I only had six. "I am the only one on that list who doesn't get leads from the company," I said. "What do I have to do so that I can be considered productive in your eyes?"

He looked at me for a few seconds, thinking. Then he said, "Well, I guess you are pacing for twelve accounts as a self-gen. That is pretty productive."

At that point, I didn't even feel like twelve was going to cut it. It seemed like the only thing I could do to get any credit around the office was to blow everyone out of the water! I decided to ramp everything up and go to war! They wanted to see me more productive? I was going to move quicker than I ever had!

The first thing I did was shadow a setter named Craig. Craig was new to our office but he was on another level of production. There were problems with his leads when it came to missing information (such as no contact info and partial addresses), but he brought the office a lot of business through sheer volume. The reason why I decided to shadow Craig is that he was doing something no one else was doing: setting appointments for the very same day he got the lead! I knew this was a valuable skill to learn, especially if I was going to ramp up my own production.

The same day track goes like this: "Mr. Jones, we're going to be in the neighborhood all day today, and we can have a specialist out by 5 p.m. with your report." Of course, this won't work all the time, but when it does, it's gold! In this industry, it is very important to have an appointment sit with the specialist/closer within three days of obtaining the lead. After three days, the chance of the appointment sitting drops off by a significant percentage. Same-day appointments, on the other hand, close at an incredibly high rate compared to a normal appointment. With this track, if the homeowner says that they can't take an appointment tonight, you follow up with, "Wonderful! Are you and the spouse normally available in the morning, afternoon, or evening? Evening? Great! I have a 6 p.m. available tomorrow. I'll send you a text now with that information, and we'll see you tomorrow!" You always assume they are available. If you give a homeowner an option, they will always push it out by two weeks, and that usually means they're not going to sit at all. If you ask, "When do you think you and the spouse will have some availability to sit down?" they will always say, "You know what, we're going to be busy for the next couple of weeks. Just give me a call in a couple of weeks, and we'll schedule something then."

The truth is that everyone has forty-five minutes to spare on any given day. They just aren't contemplating their day correctly when you put them on the spot. This means you have to help them work through it. For example, if you do accidentally ask the homeowner instead of directing the homeowner, here's how you can salvage the mistake after they say they can schedule something two weeks out. Just start by agreeing with them and say, "Absolutely, Mr. Jones! When would you say you normally get home from work? Five? Great, we have a 6 p.m. appointment available tomorrow night. Will your spouse be available as well?" Act like they never said two weeks out. This track forces the homeowner to realize that they really don't have anything better to do than watch television during that time and there's a higher chance they will take the appointment and/or sitting.

Armed with this new skill from Craig, I came out swinging! In the next two weeks, I wrote up eleven more accounts! This put my monthly total at seventeen! I was on top of the world! I had become a kind of celebrity with the setter team since I was adding setters to all my accounts. I was so excited to get some recognition at the next closer meeting and was telling all my friends and family about my success.

The month of June had been an incredibly productive month for the whole office. In the midst of the pandemic, the setter management had built up a highly productive foundation of setters and the closers were on their A game. I sat in on the next closer meeting. It was a bit of a celebration. Tom was going over the individual stats going from the top closer to the bottom. There were three closers with higher numbers than mine, and when Tom got to my name, he stopped, turned to look at me, and asked, "Matt, you got seventeen?" It's like he didn't even recognize how many deals I had been putting up. I let that get to me more than it should have. I had put everything I had into that month. Going into July, I *still* wasn't a closer despite my production. I felt like everything was wrong. Nothing made sense.

The truth is, it's always easy to criticize management from the outside but seldom does anyone understand the thought processes from the inside. That doesn't mean that you can't be right in your negative assumption, but it's always good to assume the best first.

While June was a huge month for Virginia Beach, Denver became the first office to produce over 200 accounts in a month. That was a hard pill for us to swallow. The office prestige that comes along with such milestones is incredible, and we wanted to be a part of it. "Road to 200!" still remained our vision, but the enthusiasm was no longer as great. Besides that, Salt Lake City seemed to be slipping down the leaderboards, and Las Vegas only seemed to be producing about half of their former numbers as well. I wanted to keep an eye on that.

It really does take an amazing team, especially management, to pull everything back together and rebuild during crazy times like a worldwide pandemic. It takes an incredible amount of will-power and leadership to achieve what the Virginia Beach team achieved in early to mid-2020. While I saw and felt that so many things seemed wrong, I have to admit that so much was also right and keep in mind that everything—and everyone—is a work in progress.

Chapter 2

The Lens

As I mentioned earlier, the name of the game is productivity. In every aspect of life, the more actions and the greater actions you take, the more you will succeed. By the time July 2020 rolled around, I had grinded enough to become proficient as a setter. I had also taken enough action and had just enough good advice to win over Asia. Sure, I was going for a closer or closer manager role, but a setter manager saw more of my potential than anyone else in the Virginia Beach office at the time. She contacted me fairly often to ask my opinion on one thing or another. Though, looking back, I she might have been trying to build a professional relationship.

I soon found out that Asia was being promoted. She was no longer going to be the co-setter manager of Virginia Beach. She was now going to be the Setter Director for the entire state! This meant that they needed to find someone to replace her and believe me when I say it was slim pickings. The setter team predominantly consisted of fresh-out-of-high-school kids with no real life or managerial experience. For a couple weeks, they held quite a few one-on-ones with setters who at least had an interest. One day, I stepped in the office during the one-on-ones. Justin saw me and pointed, "You want to be my co?"

I just looked at him for a second. I was thinking about how it wasn't the direction I was intending to go, but it could be my only means up in this company. "I'll entertain that," I said.

Justin looked at me, confused, "Really?!"

"Why would you ask me if you didn't think I would do it?"

The truth is, during the month of June, I earned $30,000. That's some crazy money for anyone, and I was on track to make a whole lot more. Justin knew this, and he also knew that I would be taking a bit of a pay cut if I moved over. The truth is, I personally am not fulfilled by selling deals. I'm good at it, but I get so much more enjoyment from developing people. Sales did not come naturally to me by any stretch of the imagination, so through all of my struggle, striving, and pushing through, I developed good methods for understanding and teaching sales.

My first sales job was for La-Z-Boy Furniture when I lived in the Bay Area of California in a city called Santa Rosa. Before La-Z-Boy, I was the Assistant General Manager for an Applebee's making $55,000 a year. Anyone who lives in the Bay Area of California knows that's not enough money to live on. I felt like I had hit a ceiling. Even if I worked my way to a general manager position, I would be topping out at $70,000 if I stayed at Applebee's. So I decided to take a leap of faith. I had never tried a 100 percent commission job before because of the onus being on my personal production. But I also knew that mindset was weak, and I needed to prove that I could take on anything.

The La-Z-Boy in Santa Rosa was one of the top-producing stores in the nation. Normally, they would never take on someone with no sales experience, but if there's anything I excel at, it's a job interview. They took a chance on me, and I dove in! I learned all the furniture jargon and the model codes. I spent time with the store designer to get a better grasp on how colors, textures, and patterns work together. I learned every bit of information I could as fast as I could in an attempt to make myself as ready as possible to take on this industry. Turns out, I was pretty terrible. They say that if you've never been in sales, it takes you about six months to get some traction. I didn't have six months. My monthly overhead was approximately $4,500, and each month I was bringing in about $2,000. I couldn't understand how my coworkers were making $6,000 to $10,000 a month and why I was so far behind. I broke down crying multiple times at this job. I contemplated quitting and cutting my losses multiple times, but I don't think that I could live with the thought that I couldn't survive in a sales environment. I knew that if I could just find a missing puzzle piece or something, I would change my life—possibly forever. I decided that I needed to push through. I knew that if someone else had figured it out, I could get there. I just needed a quicker route to get there.

I've never been one for reading, but I felt like I had no other option. A friend recommended *How to Win Friends and Influence People* by Dale Carnegie. You know, the first book that every salesperson on the planet has read. And I followed suit. I read that book, highlighted, outlined. I put the things I was learning into practice and started seeing an immediate difference! Of course, my main problem was that I was trying to sell with information. Most people don't purchase logically; they purchase emotionally when it comes to expensive things. Understanding emotional selling is a turning point in the career of any beginning salesperson.

I didn't get any traction until I was eight months into working at La-Z-Boy, but after that eighth month, I rapidly progressed. The following year, I went on to be in the top 3 percent of La-Z-Boy salespeople nationwide. After that second year, I felt like I had hit a ceiling once again. In case you haven't noticed, I don't like ceilings. Any time I feel like there's no progress left to be made, I don't feel comfortable anymore. If I had a dream job, it would be one with no ceiling where I could constantly progress and earn more as time goes on.

Feeling like I had hit a ceiling, I decided to move to a state where my money would go further. I'm still so incredibly grateful to the La-Z-Boy owners and management who gave me a chance, as well as one crazy coworker who always pushed me to my limits.

The reason why I tell that story is because, in both cases—learning to be a salesman and learning to be a setter—I fell on my face. I learned slower than most, but I pushed through. This has given me a different perspective on how to better train new and struggling individuals, and that's a strength I have a passion for sharing. That is also why the setter manager position interested me. I could constantly work with people who have little to no experience and help them move up the ladder.

Although at first it sounded like they were offering me the job, that wasn't actually the case. They wanted me to compete for the position. This, of course, I thought was crazy! Why would anyone ask me to leave a coveted position (and the money I was making) to compete against a setter? I felt like I was taking crazy pills! My response was, "If you think I've been consistent and am the right person for the job, then hire me. If you don't, then don't. I'm not going to play the Hunger Games for a few weeks in order to get a promotion." This is a sales technique. I was attempting to reframe the conversation. They wanted me to compete for four weeks for the position, and I was saying, correctly, that anyone can crush it for four weeks. Prior consistency is the barometer that should be used for such an important position.

Let's break down that style of thinking for a moment. Say you have a few different people who have worked in the same role for a decent amount of time. Each individual person illustrates decent skills for a management position. If you look back through their time at the company and examine their consistent patterns and work ethic, that's what you're getting as a manager. On the other hand, if you say, "Let's see what you can do in the next month," you will get high levels of work, and sometimes even different styles of work—but only for that month. You may think someone has really stepped up. However, once that person is selected for the spot, they will immediately revert to their consistent form of working. Upper management might get frustrated with this result because they were focusing heavily on that one month, hoping that they were going to get "the one" unrealistic manager.

The style of promotion that involves heavy focus on a short period of time incentivizes "playing the game," which can be confusing if the stated ethos of the environment is to "trust the process." If the thing that is said doesn't match what is practiced, you end up with confusion. Most people don't recognize just how important this is, but even if the confusion is on a psychological or subconscious level, living up to company promises is one of the most important practices that permeates office culture. The company promises don't mean anything without an environment that supports those promises. I cover this in more detail later in the book.

In any case, "trust the process" refers to a constant striving for personal growth. If you are constantly reading, listening to podcasts, and putting teachings into practice, your mindset will change. When your mindset changes, that bleeds into all aspects of your life, and you become a better person in general fairly rapidly. This is an amazing practice to instill in your team. Everyone moves at a different pace, but if everyone is moving in the right direction, the team is constantly improving.

On the other hand, "playing the game" is to be the right person in the right place at the right time. This is something anyone can do, especially if they're a careerist. Someone who plays the game has no need to expand on anything, innovate, or find new or better methods for future business. Playing the game is doing exactly what you were told to do in overdrive mode. Playing the game is showing that you can do one thing at a crazy high level in order to attain a promotion. You want to see me knock on doors for a month? I'll put up some crazy numbers that will turn heads. But again, if that isn't something I prioritize, the moment I get that promotion, I will revert back to my normal management style. In my head, my style is correct. Anyone can fake it for a short amount of time, but it doesn't last long in the day to day.

It's always important for us as sales managers and leaders to understand exactly what we are incentivizing when we create plans and structures. The underlying psychological effects of the actions we take and the procedures we make have significant repercussions for the individuals in question, as well as how the team overall views management. Unfortunately, I have known quite a few egotistical managers personally and have read quite a few books that describe managers who have so much ego that they can't be bothered by what the team thinks. They think of the team members just as people who work for them.

Humility is a very important characteristic to practice if you want a strong office culture. Even if people are not currently on our level, they are on track. If we pull the track from under them or hold them down, we are doing a disservice to them, ourselves, and our team.

Coming back to the story, a week after I had turned down the option to compete, Chad sat down with me. He asked if I had thought about the setter manager position. I told him, "Look, if you guys want me to take it, I already said I would."

Of course, Chad referred back to the previous option. They wanted me to compete. By now, I knew that they really wanted me for that job, so I wasn't in a rush to follow rules I didn't agree with.

Two more weeks went by, and then I was asked to lunch by Asia and Tom. They tried a different approach, this time giving me two options. Tom said that I could finally be a full-fledged closer or that I could go back to being a setter. This is a good trick to see where someone's heart is at. Who wouldn't take the coveted closer position? Turns out, I'm that person. I agreed to go back to being a setter. I was somewhat terrified because, again, I had been terrible at being a setter before. But by now, I also knew that I could handle it. If I couldn't, I really didn't have any business managing that department anyways.

One day, after going back to being a setter, I was pulled into the manager's office. They asked me to sit down with two other setters. "You are the three people we are looking at for the position," Asia said. One of the other setters was named Corey. Corey was very proficient at his job with an astoundingly high close rate on his leads. When closers went to his houses, the homeowners often would greet them with, "How do we sign up?" Corey, however, had only been working at ION for three weeks, so I knew that wasn't happening. It was a carrot on a string.

Ryan (the third setter being considered), on the other hand, was a strong personality and he brought results consistently. He is strong competition whether he's shooting for a position or chasing the hot waitress at the local Mexican restaurant. He would take a challenge anywhere, even when it gets him into trouble.

The thing about Ryan is that he is incredibly good at raising the ceiling. See, when it comes to office production, you have to be mindful of two things: raising the ceiling and raising the floor. Raising the ceiling is motivating your top producers to produce on a higher level. This is predominantly done through competition. It is also equally important to raise the floor with support and training. If a new recruit can't get their "sea legs" and find a little success quick enough in a sales environment, they will be gone fairly quick. The issue with Ryan was that he is so incredibly competitive and brash that he can motivate the top producers to work an extra 10 percent but when he does, the floor distances themselves and becomes bitter. I'm the antithesis of that. I focus entirely on the floor and don't motivate the ceiling very much at all.

While Asia and Justin weren't too sure about Ryan, they were equally unsure about me because of my frustration. If I don't understand the reason for something, I generally require explanations. And if I don't agree with the way things are done, I am vocal about it. I'm not the best communicator. Also, no management team is comfortable with someone coming in who already has the desire to start changing things.

At the time they told the three of us we were competing for the position, I had decided to forget about the manager role and work on developing new recruits.

A new setter reached out to me around this time. Her name was Hailey. She was young, only about twenty-three years old. She had been working at ION for a month or two; however, she only produced about three appointments per week, so she was very underestimated. She asked to shadow me for a bit to see how I do things.

I'm a fairly analytical person, and I like to understand the inner workings and psychology of everything. It helps me forecast and understand my options. So, when people shadow me, they hear me say "The psychology behind this is ..." fairly often. Normally, not too many people entirely understand where I'm coming from, but Hailey did. She really followed how I broke everything down and put it into practice fast. I spent about two weeks with her—every day, one-on-one, watching her improve and really understand all aspects of setting. There was, however, one area in which I don't teach well. We call it the transition.

Setters in all industries have a pitch. The pitch is designed to provoke just enough interest for the homeowner to take an appointment. The transition is asking for the necessary information and appointment time for the homeowner to commit to. It's the hardest part for most setters. It's generally uncomfortable to ask something like this within two minutes of meeting them, but again, it's best to guide their decision.

I asked Justin to help her with that one aspect. Justin has absolutely no problem telling a homeowner to do something. Justin also likes to argue. He enjoys it. I knew if anyone could help her learn the transition quickly, it was him. They spent one day together. The next day, Hailey went out on her own and generated eight appointments! Our group feed was lit up with Hailey's appointments. Everyone was turning their heads! She was a relatively unknown worker who became the newest hot topic at the office in the course of a day. That week she went on to generate twenty-two appointments. This was a huge benefit to me because she made me look amazing. Upper management paraded her around, as they tend to do with anyone who is crushing it. And every single time, she mentioned me. I gained a lot of recognition for my training skills and that is what sealed it for me.

After that, setters constantly asked me to come watch them on the doors. Every setter joins the company dreaming of having the ability to produce twenty leads a week. Normally, no one works hard enough to produce half that. People join sales companies because they hear about the earning potential, but the learning curve is so steep, and our natural disposition to be lazy keeps us from working full-time hours. Because of this, sales companies are naturally revolving doors when it comes to recruitment. If you hire five people, maybe one will stay longer than a month. This is why most sales companies don't have anyone fill out applications or bring in resumes. Hire everyone and see who sticks! Sometimes a high-caliber salesperson with over ten years of experience will come in and fail. Other times, someone will come straight from Starbucks and crush everyone else! If you put in the effort, it doesn't matter where you came from.

If you want to be a successful setter, work the hours. We always say that if you put in at least thirty-six hours a week, you will make six figures just knocking on doors and setting appointments. If you work six days a week for six hours a day, you should generate at least two appointments per day and twelve appointments per week. Here's the issue. If a setter knocks for one hour and generates two appointments, that setter will usually say "job well done" and head home because they completed their daily goal. Then they will come out the next day, work two hours without generating a lead, get discouraged, and go home. Now they're only acquiring one lead per day. This is why we say work the hours. The goal shouldn't be two leads a day; it should be six hours a day. Treat it like a normal job where you clock in and clock out. It's interesting that when someone works a nine-to-five job, they will clock in on time and clock out on time so they aren't fired. But for a sales job where you have the ability to make far more money and create your own schedule, the moment we feel success or failure, we call it. If you work the hours, however, it's far more sustainable. Let's go back to the first day. Say after the setter generated two leads in the first hour, they decided to work the next five. Maybe that setter would end the day with five appointments. The next day, when they had nothing in the first two hours, maybe they worked the next four hours and only generated one appointment. Now that setter has three times the number of leads because they worked the hours! Even if a setter works a full day and comes home without an appointment, they are not empty-handed and should not be discouraged. They now have six hours of experience they didn't have before, and that is something to be proud of.

The reason why we naturally call it quits at the first sign of success or failure is due to internal resistance. There's a great book about resistance called *The War of Art* by Steven Pressfield. I highly recommend this book as I have read it multiple times. Resistance is the voice in our head that points us toward immediate gratification. For example, I might wake up ready to knock but then I see it's pretty cold outside. I think maybe I'll get out tomorrow. Or I see it's raining, and I think I'll just wait around and see if it clears up. Or maybe it's getting dark out, and I think no one's going to want me knocking on their door. Or I've been knocking two hours and have nothing, and I think I should try again tomorrow.

Have you had these thoughts? Our mind is constantly trying to weasel its way out of working. The problem is that instant gratification prolongs any meaningful, long-term growth. Meaningful long-term growth is the process! That's what we should be chasing in life! We have to deal with the same resistance when it comes to things like diets and quitting vices as well. We need to learn to work through it. It's not easy, but as I've said before, everyone is a work in progress. We need to hear that voice and accept a challenge! We need to hear that voice and understand that we're not just anyone else! It's cold outside? Guess what? I bet no one else in any other company is out there knocking. That's what separates me from them. It's raining? More for me! In fact, most homeowners will listen out of pity just because I'm knocking in the rain. Who else is doing that? No one, that's who! It's getting dark? I'm just maximizing my hours, and that's why I'm successful! There's no such thing as a bad neighborhood. I'm here to help people, and everyone needs to know what I have for them! Mindset is everything!

The Virginia Beach office has a "process." Here the management often says, "Be naive enough to trust the process." Of course, I'm not a huge fan of that wording. I considered myself curious enough to follow the process. No one explains or has a definition of what that process is, but it is rooted in self-improvement. There is strong encouragement for workers to read, work out, learn how to have work–life balance, etc. The idea is that if you continuously improve your mindset, perspectives, and actions, those things will bleed into your work, as well as every other aspect of your life. You will notice yourself quickly evolving into a better version of yourself. It's a never-ending process. It's interesting to work for a company that is working toward empowering people rather than just seeing them as a means for production.

All this being said seemed to be just that: said. There seemed to be a blind spot when it came to new and struggling setters. You would hear the positivity, but the support wasn't entirely there. This, of course, is why setters were reaching out to me. There was a need for in-depth training in order for setters to get some traction so they could make just enough money to survive long enough to get good at the job. As I mentioned in the previous chapter, I was in the same boat when I started.

At this point, when I had started spending a significant amount of time training new setters, I was finally offered the setter manager position. I couldn't wait to see where I would fit in. The funny thing is that for every job I had taken before, I made sure I was proficient at the job, I dressed the part, and I acted the part before taking the job. This way I could move in seamlessly. This was the first promotion where I knew I didn't quite understand the full job but I was excited to see what kind of manager I would become.

Many years ago, I was listening to a biblical lecture by a professor named Jordan Peterson. In that lecture, he provided interesting insight into the concept of confusion. "Confusion happens when what is supposed to be real and what is actually real are not the same." That's a definition that has stuck with me all this time. Of course, my first takeaway was that I don't care what people say; I care what people do. People can say something that makes them look positive or can spin things in a positive way, but when you see how they act and react, you see how they actually think. The downside about this line of thinking was that I believed everything to be intentional when that isn't always the case. There are plenty of times we don't even realize we say something that doesn't line up with our actions or crafted management structures.

In any case, I was beginning to take this same definition and notice where there were office and cultural promises and sayings that didn't line up with the way things are actually done. This means that confusion lies within the fundamental levels of the office ethos. It's like if you had a horse, and it's a really strong horse. This horse has taken you everywhere you need to go and you are so proud of this horse. It's better than all the other horses.

Then you notice that it's actually been sick this entire time. You may say, "Hey, it's still better than everything else," or you may want to see what that horse is really, truly capable of if you could make it well.

I wanted to see the latter.

Chapter 3:

Incentivizing Behavior

nheriting the management position wasn't as easy or seamless as I had imagined it would be. This was partially because of cultural issues, which I will touch on later, and partially because of the manner in which we had been incentivizing our team. However, the most immediate issue was micromanagement.

The Virginia Beach office is a powerhouse office that was built from the ground up in the two years before I started working there. Chad and Tom were there from the very beginning and went through hell in order to get the office to being even remotely profitable. For a while, Chad even lived in the office without anyone knowing it to help save money. This is an office that sells solar panels in a state that didn't know the first thing about solar before they showed up here. So these guys had to educate everyone and hope that someone would take a shot on solar, even though no one around had it at the time. That is a hard market to break in to.

Asia and Justin came a little later, but the setter organization was brand-new to the company when they did. Together they helped build the structures that the full company would later adopt. This office was their baby. And when you work that hard and that long to make something successful, sometimes it's hard to step back and let the next person take over. This can be an issue for the next manager. Say you were the one who built the office. You went through all the hardships, tried different processes, and created structures that worked and got you to this point. Just because those structures got you doesn't mean they will get you to the next level. We have a tendency to find the best horse and ride it as far as we can, but when that horse won't go any farther, it's nearly impossible for us to let it go. So, if we maintain a stranglehold on office management, we are not allowing new ideas and innovation that could take us to the next level. It is a very hard thing to accept that the only consistent thing is change. We must always be open to change.

When I started the setter manager role, my first job was just to see where I fit in. I thought it should be easy. As a co-manager, all of the setter meetings were ran by me and Justin. Of course, I wanted to make the most of what I have, so I was always prepared with a lesson plan or something. However, the first meeting was a little strange. Every manager inside and above the office was there—not to watch but to maintain their stranglehold. A meeting meant to be run by me and Justin included Tom, Chad, Asia, and Jordan (someone who was replacing Chad due to promotions) all chiming in and taking over the meeting with their ideas and teachings. I found myself a wallflower and simply pulled up a chair and sat with the rest of the class. There was no room for me here. There was certainly no room for me to grow as a manager.

For two weeks, these meetings went on the exact same way. I never had room to talk in the meetings that I was technically supposed to be running. The environment was suffocating every opportunity I had to become the manager they needed. How could the previous managers even begin to focus on their new work if I never had the ability to take over my new role?

If you haven't caught on by now, I'm not someone to be quiet about anything really. I complain a lot. I am very aware of that, but if I don't vocalize what I am not okay with, I have to be okay with the way things currently are. So, I let the rest of the management know exactly how negative the environment was and that I needed them to step back or not be present at my meetings. Thankfully, they understood immediately and allowed me to take over from there.

Everyone needs room to grow. Everyone is going to make mistakes. We can't worry about the repercussions or fallout from mistakes we make. In fact, most of the time, there will never be an issue. There will just be an opportunity to learn and grow. If we allow people develop with enough space and creative control, we are going to find new and exciting ways of seeing and teaching that we have never found before. Every manager has something unique to bring to the table as long as they have the breathing room and creative control to expand on their ideas. If they don't have that space, they're not going to be excited about their work. If they're not excited about their work, the class isn't going to be excited either.

In a way, this reminds me of the overprotection of children in school with anti-bullying campaigns that came through and told everyone not to say mean things to each other or bully each other.

There was a hard push to sanitize reality so that children didn't have to encounter or understand hardship. This can be a very dangerous proposition considering school is the first time most children will explore social hierarchies and even begin to navigate them. If we sanitize children and guard them from social negatives, we prolong their understanding and growth for the real world. As parents, we don't need to micromanage them and their interactions but rather help them better navigate situations the next time they encounter them. We are guides who can give them room to grow, develop, and understand. The same is true for workers.

Now there was also an issue with how we incentivized our workers. "Fall in love with the process, not the results." This is a quote you hear time and time again in all sales companies. This quote is very true. If you love the process and really understand it intimately, if you grind constantly, the results will come to you. But if you focus on the results, you have a tendency to fail. Say, for instance, you're sitting down with a potential customer and you are trying to sell them on a product. If you come from a place of trying to help the customer make the right choice for them and their family, you are going to do well. But if you are thinking about how you really need the money from the sale, every potential customer will feel that desperation from you. No one will buy from you when you are too focused on the result.

Another very common occurrence that comes from loving the result is going through a dry spell. Now this happens to everyone, even if they are a "love the process" type of worker. However, if we go a day or two without success, we often wonder what we are doing wrong or doing differently. We shift our focus to finding the result. We push harder, try from different angles, get people to come watch us and give us feedback about what we're doing wrong when what's wrong is the focus. Having the wrong focus can easily turn two days of no results into a full week of no results. That's why I tell everyone that the best thing to do during a dry spell is relax, act like nothing matters, and go about your work as if there are no results to be had. Just knock on the doors, talk to people, and try not to care about the results. Once you get your first lead out of the dry spell, the rest will come back to you. Love the process.

The truth is that money, in general, is a bad motivator. If you are not making enough money, you will reek of desperation. With that logic, you would think that if you were making plenty of money, you would continue to work better. However, normally if someone is making more money than they actually need, they become complacent, start cutting corners, and only focus on the low-hanging fruit. That's why it's best to find people who aren't motivated by money—unless that number is unreasonably high, in which case, great! It's always good to be unreasonable with monetary goals. It's best, however, to find people who want to master the process, or who can shift their motivation to the process side and away from the results side. It's even better to have someone buy into a culture and vision that is bigger than themselves, which is another crucial concept that I go into later in this book.

In August 2020, two months before I became a manager, the office had its best month of the year. We had finally broken the 200 sales in a month mark! It was something we had been fighting for all year, and it was finally achieved. However, during this month, I began documenting the way the setter organization was incentivized. Every so often, say once a week, there was a new cash incentive to get setters motivated to go knock on doors. It sounds awesome considering most companies don't pay nearly as much as this company does. You would think with all the money being thrown around it would be like being in one of those money tornado booths. You see someone in one of those and they're doing anything they can to grab the paper swirling around them. However, I noticed a common theme with the incentives.

Each incentive would only pay the top producer in a certain area. Say, for example, whoever had the most leads generated in one day would get an extra $100 or whoever had the most appointments held in one week would get an extra $300. Naturally, this type of incentive sounds like a good idea because, in theory, you get your team to compete and work harder. But just because something *should* work doesn't mean it *does* work.

Here is the issue with the incentives. We had a setter team of twenty-two people. Some were veterans, and some were brand-new. Some were killing it, and some were struggling. Some were normally killing it but were going through a rough patch. At the time, we had three setters who were produced at a high level every single week. These are the kind of setters companies would kill to have. It's all about work ethic with these three people. But perception is everything. Whenever we had an incentive to produce the most of something, those three people would get excited and produce approximately 10 percent more than usual. The other nineteen, however, would hear about the incentive and immediately became disincentivized and give up! They knew that there was no possible way, no matter how hard they tried, that they could win that money. (That, of course, isn't true at all, but that's how perception works.) So, the top few setters would work a little bit harder while the rest of the team was working quite a bit less because they were disincentivized. We were paying crazy amounts of money for our team to produce less overall! Every time we put out a results-driven incentive, we were paying more for net negative appointments!

I brought this up to Asia and mentioned that we were incentivizing so often with so much money that the incentives didn't even seem like incentives anymore. They were just a normal part of the job. I maintained that if we cut all incentives for an entire month, we would see an increase in the whole team's production. Naturally, considering the office had just had its best month ever, Asia didn't agree with me. She wanted to go the opposite direction. "Next month we're going to ramp up the incentives!" she said. Of course, I wanted to try my idea just to at least see the results, but if my theory was correct, the next month would fall behind.

During September, our office had incentives on top of incentives—new incentives every day or every other day on top of weekly incentives. It was a mess. It was also fairly difficult to follow and track all the incentives. I'll tell you this much—the top setters were getting their pockets lined with cash. Sometimes they didn't even realize they had won an incentive considering how frequent they were. That month, the setter managers spent the entire office budget for the month of September and nearly all the office budget for October. That same month, setter production was down 10 percent and the closer production was down 20 percent. While the closer team wasn't part of the incentives, the setter team was in charge of setting quality appointments for the closer team.

Considering we were left with very little money to work with in October, I got to try out my methods as I was coming into management. We got to see the methods back-to-back in a two-month period.

"Fall in love with the process, not the results."

We talk about falling in love with the process so often in this industry but we don't really embrace the idea. Think about the subconscious confusion companies create when they say this over and over and over again, but they only incentivize the results—and not the process. Really think about that for a second. Think about the confusion of having a manager standing in front of a class saying, "You all need to fall in love the process, not the results. If you love the process, the results will come. Trust me." And then follow that up with, "Whoever gets the most results for me today gets $200!" You show what you really value with your actions. You may say it's the process that's important, but your actions clearly show that you value results more. If we incentivize the behavior we want from our team rather than whoever does the most of something, everyone is going to be better at their job. If everyone is progressively getting better at their job, the results will come tenfold! If we want our setters to work longer hours, let's incentivize time spent knocking on doors. If we want our team to work in the dark, let's incentivize working late. It's a simple concept with a vast amount of material to work with! Just matching words to actions will free up some of the underlying confusion in the office. That's what I'm talking about! It's like we're untangling cords here!

Luckily for me, this was a concept that Chad understood quickly, and we put it to work immediately. Again, in the month of October, we didn't really have much money to work with. I was totally okay with that considering I wanted to see how the team would work without incentives. I did, however, want to try out the new concept of behavioral incentives, so it was time to get creative. We asked what behavior we wanted to instill during the month of October. Justin used a genius saying that time of the year: "It's not late, it's just dark." He always uses this saying toward the last quarter of the year because it started getting darker earlier and most setters would likely go home early. That was the perfect behavior. Now we had to turn that into an incentive. At the time, sunset was at 6:22 p.m., so we made the incentive for working after 6:30 p.m. This, of course, required us to verify that they were working after 6:30 p.m. Also, we didn't have much money to work with and we wanted to move away from disincentivizing the majority of the team.

Jordan had a fantastic idea. "Buy a TV," he said. "Buy a TV and leave it in the front of the office so everyone sees it at every meeting." It was an awesome idea! Everyone wants a TV. And to get everyone to participate, we made it a raffle! That way, no matter how productive someone is, everyone has a chance of winning. Below is the incentive we created.

It's Not Late, It's Just Dark!

If you generate a lead after 6:30 p.m., post a selfie with the homeowner in our GroupMe feed. Caption the selfie with "It's not late, it's just dark!" For each of these generated correctly, the setter will receive a raffle ticket.

This was a hit! For the next two weeks, our group feed was blowing up with selfies with homeowners in the dark. The best part was, every time a selfie was posted after 6:30 p.m., the setter captioned it, "It's not late, it's just dark." Because of this, all the setters who decided to stay home or go home early had to constantly see their peers being successful in the dark saying the same line over and over again: "It's not late, it's just dark." At the end of the month, we raffled off the TV, and the person who won it only had one ticket. While most people wouldn't like that, I loved it! I knew that it would show everyone that they all had a chance to win incentives here! That incentive only cost us $400 while our monthly office budget was normally $3,000. For the month of

October, our setter numbers went up 17.5 percent and, to this day, we often see setters posting appointments in our group feed saying, "It's not late, it's just dark" even though there isn't an incentive for it anymore. That is the behavior we were trying to create.

The success of this incentive led to the whole management team coming up with tons of ideas. We worked on full programs that we issued statewide, although it's always good to be mindful of how often you have incentives. If you do them too often, they will lose their meaning and setters will become disinterested. Keep incentives special.

The criteria we now use for constructing incentives goes like this. First, incentives must be proactive, not reactive. This is a very important thing to understand. Say, for example, you're having a down day. The team just isn't producing. Maybe they haven't even gone out to work and 4 p.m. rolls by. Quite often a manager will look at how low their stats are for the day and make a quick incentive decision: $100 for whoever gets the most leads between 5 and 8 p.m.! I've seen that one quite often. This is a reactive incentive. The chances of you coaxing someone to get out on the doors for the next couple hours are very small. If it doesn't increase the daily numbers, the team sees you as desperate, and they are less likely to work hard the next day. In this scenario, it is much better to cut your losses for that day and prepare for the next. Put together an incentive plan for the next day. Considering everyone should be rested from not working the day before, there's a high probability you can incentivize them to work super hard the following day. It's even better if you plan out the incentives to be proactive and aligned with what you are forecasting for that month or the next month. If it is going to start snowing, make the prizes winter gear so they can work in the cold. If certain people are having a hard time making friends, pair them up for an incentive. Always be looking ahead to see what can most benefit your team.

Second, the incentives must be constructed to incentivize a desired behavior instead of just a result. This way we can actively have our team self-improving during their daily work.

Third, the winner shouldn't always be the most productive person. We want everyone to participate, so it is better to let everyone have a shot at winning prizes regardless of how far along they are as a setter. We're a team. We're all in this together.

Fourth, the incentives can be constructed in a way that obtains valuable information from the setter team. This was an idea that came later. For our December 2020 incentive, Chad came up with a good idea. He noticed that we had about thirty setters but only fourteen were working on any given day. He figured if we could just get them knocking on doors, they would produce. The hard part was just getting everyone on the doors. With this concept in mind, I constructed a month-long incentive called Winter Warriors. I divided the setters into groups of three and had them take selfies on the doors early and late in the day as a team. Each selfie was worth one point. Selfies were worth two points on Saturday and if a team hit a certain threshold for production for the week, they doubled their weekly points.

Of course, with a month-long setup, there had to be a fantastic prize, so each member of the winning team would earn a PlayStation 5. I also assigned the teams so we could have people working together who could learn from each other. For example, I paired someone who had low confidence with someone overflowing with confidence. I paired someone who didn't like to work in the dark with someone who always worked in the dark. Don't shy away from being creative. If you see an opportunity, find a way to turn it into a game.

When I said we obtained information from an incentive, what we took away from this one is that a lot of people really wanted that PlayStation. I wanted to see who would let their team down. Who would stay home and not take the selfies to the detriment of their peers? That is a good way to tell who has really bought into the office culture. That doesn't necessarily mean that a setter is a bad person or is someone to give up on or cut ties with. It may be our fault as managers. A good leader should be able to find a way for everyone to be a part of the culture.

Also, incentivizing behavior doesn't always have to come in the form of a game. There are many different, even free, ways of doing this. Depending on your office budget, sometimes you will have to get creative.

One easy way of achieving this is through speech. Sometimes if I have an incentive plan queued up for next month, I will change the words I use in the month prior to ease into the transition. For example, if I want to incentivize teamwork, I will start using words and phrases that refer to us as a team. It's always good to keep a setter team hyped with energy, so we often yell things collectively. If we are focusing on teamwork, we can get the group to collectively yell something like "Team VB!" at the end of a meeting or I can refer to the team as a "Solar Army" or maybe say that we're going to "have a solar party in the streets!" This may not sound like much, but it's a free, subconscious way of making us think like a team.

We can also have a common enemy. I don't do this anymore because I don't like to compare us to other offices. However, when we used to be neck and neck with other offices, we would constantly yell, "Beat Denver!" We can also stop referring to individuals at meetings and only refer to the team.

You can also incentivize behavior through office decor. Every sales office has decor with famous sales lines or possibly an acronym for words like "success." I believe it's good to have many different signs and canvasses that can be switched out. Keep the office visually interesting. Your team will constantly be looking at new sayings that may hit them differently the second time around. If you are trying to incentivize a behavior or mindset that month, change the decor to all the things you have that best fit that narrative. Sure, it's a little extra money, but you're investing in every individual on your team and it will pay for itself thousands of times over.

One of my favorite ways—and one of the most important—of incentivizing behavior is also one of the most overlooked things by managers. And guess what? It's also free. I say managers, but really this is a difference between managers and leaders. Leaders must be aware of how they talk to and treat their team. They need to be aware of how what they say is being taken by the group. This is also incredibly important to the office culture, which, in my opinion, is the most important thing for office production. Quite often, when managers want their team to do certain things, they bring up these things over and over and shame the team or individuals for not doing these things. Or if there's an issue with the team working in general, I have seen managers have a meeting and come down on the group, saying, "You all need to be out there working! What do I have to do to get you guys motivated? I can generate however many leads in a day, why can't you?"

Has that approach ever worked? I haven't seen that work. In fact, I have only seen that disincentivize teams and individuals. So why do we keep going back to it?

The truth is, if you treat your team like children, you're going to have a room full of children. If you treat your team like professionals, you're going to have a room full of professionals. In fact, I have made it a point never to tell my team what to do or what they should be doing. I will also refer to them as professionals even when they are working poorly, saying things like, "We are all professional door-knockers, we need to get back to confirming all of our appointments." Using phrases like this connects the idea of confirming appointments to being professional, and everyone wants to think of themselves as professional. You can use that technique in so many ways.

The point is, so many managers are brash because they don't understand how to communicate with their team in a way that works. In their mind, they think something *should* work. I've had other managers come to me saying that something they're doing *should* work but that doesn't mean that it *does* work, and I'm only interested in what *does* work.

People generally get into management because they've developed a drive that pushes them further than the rest of their peers—at least in the door-to-door industry. The problem is that most people will not see the same things or understand the same ideas and concepts as you. So things that *should* work might work for you but not for the people on your team. Sometimes we have to meet people where they're at and bring them up over time.

That brings me to the next super powerful form of incentivizing behavior—coaching. Coaching takes time and patience, which is why it's never used as much as it should be. We're all on different levels and, unfortunately, that means there's a disconnect where we don't understand things the same way as other people. In fact, one of the most difficult parts of "the process" for me is understanding how to communicate my ideas to someone who hasn't followed the same steps or read the same books as me. If I just tell people what's happening and why, most people don't understand concepts that seem so clear to me. As managers, we are required to come down to others' level and learn to communicate in a way that makes sense to them. I'm sure someone reading this is thinking I really am crazy, but I'll explain this in greater detail later on. Currently, I read five books a month. That is fairly recent, and I was pretty against reading for most of my adult life. In fact, the reason I read so much now is because I was on the receiving end of some very important coaching.

We had a setter who was causing quite an issue in the office. He was a very talented and highly productive setter, so we tolerated him quite a bit. Unfortunately, his behavior was fairly toxic. He was constantly a disruption during meetings, sometimes to the point of taking over. He always believed he had the right methods for everything and that we were teaching all the wrong things and was very vocal about it. He was fairly disrespectful. At one point, he even tried to petition other setters to create a counterculture against the management team and said that he would be their voice, saying that we didn't treat them or teach them well. He succeeded in getting a few high-level setters to be disruptive and disrespectful and, soon after, many setters even stopped showing up to meetings. Veteran setters didn't want to be in such a negative environment. Our office culture was horrifying, and there was no real motivation for our team. We were fractured.

The interesting thing is that Justin saw this coming from a mile away. No one else saw this coming. Like I said earlier, Justin's management style is to run a tight ship using fear. The company never allow Justin to manage the way he wanted to; he was required to adopt the management style that he followed. The problem with the adopted management style is that it was compassionate and patient to a fault. We had zero accountability and let everyone do and act any way they wanted. We gave everyone a second, third, fourth, and tenth chance!

Our idea, like anyone else, was that we needed to fire the setter who was creating problems. Seems simple enough, right? But our company doesn't really work like that. Justin and I appealed to upper management to let them know that we wanted to cut ties with this individual. They wanted to discuss it.

Chad and Asia invited me and Justin out to lunch. They wanted us to discuss in depth the issues we were having with this setter and our plan of action. This conversation was strange since it was mainly me and Justin doing all the talking. Chad and Asia's approach was incredibly Socratic as they had us expand on certain elements of ideas we were talking about. Justin and I had a game plan ready, but I was getting the feeling that the others didn't approve, although they wouldn't give us an alternative. After a fairly long three hours, I had a light-bulb moment! Then Justin had the same light-bulb moment! "It's not that we need to cut the head off the snake; we need to construct an environment where no one can become a snake!"

Chad and Asia smiled, and that wrapped things up. I then realized that they had that conclusion ready when they came in, and it was strange to me. "If that's what you wanted us to understand, why wouldn't you just tell us?" I asked.

Asia responded, "We needed you to come to that conclusion on your own."

Have you ever had a moment where you felt like you were on top of the world, but in an instant, you have a clear understanding that you are so far behind that it shakes you to your core? That's how I felt right then. It hit me that I really didn't know anything. That is a hard brick wall to hit. I then came to the conclusion that I needed to do what they were actively doing in order to get to the next level. I needed to read books! I immediately began cutting television time in order to make sure I could read a decent amount every month. The next month, I read five books and quickly realized two things:

1. I didn't have a deep well of teachings to draw from. Reading is how I fill that well.
2. My perspectives are profoundly changing more quickly than they ever had before. I needed to do this in order to be the right leader to bring my team into the new phases of the company.

Reading is easily the best investment I've ever made in myself. It is much more noticeable now in my teachings.

Do you see how this form of coaching had such a powerful impact on my behavior? The patience and understanding required to bring someone to your way of thinking is an incredibly powerful tool, especially when you're dealing with other management. Even though I'm rarely on the same page as anyone else, I'm incredibly grateful for the leadership that inspires me.

That's how you incentivize behavior.

Chapter 4:

Creative Control

s it enough for a manager to simply fill a position? Is it enough for a high-caliber individual to work solely from an old template? Is it enough for the human spirit to be bound to the concepts and ideas of the leaders above them? Should concepts and ideas bind anyone? Can an office be taken to the next level while complying with the vestigial practices that helped build it? Can an office even begin to truly evolve if forced to hold on to the relics of how the industry has always been?

We can only take an office as far as we can see. If concepts and ideas are the word and the gospel, doesn't that incentivize managers to keep a narrow vision? How important is creative control to any manager? The truth is that it brings life back to your spirit. Technically I don't mean this in a spiritual sense, though you can take it that way if you'd like. I mean it more in the sense of going from the dull and the mundane to having your eyes light up with excitement!

Besides, sales are often defined as the transfer of belief from one person to another. Doesn't that also apply to management addressing their team? How excited can you possibly be if you are simply filling a position?

As I mentioned before, sometimes offices are relatively new and it took a very special person to build it from the ground up, including the structure and processes that make the office run. When it is time for that special person to move up, of course, they want to teach the next person all the things to be successful at the job. That's wonderful, but it should be considered a jumping-off point for the new person. Unfortunately, we have a strong habit of not letting go when we leave. We always want to check in and make sure they're doing everything "right," and this can easily turn into micromanaging. It's like we never left. When you don't hold that position anymore, let it go! Of course, we should always be there for coaching and advice; however, mistakes are an important part of any job—and life in general—for growth.

Micromanaging the new person, we might not even be witnessing mistakes but something we don't understand yet. One of the chapters in Jordan Peterson's book, *12 Rules for Life* is titled: "Assume that the person you are listening to might know something you don't." This is one of my favorite books. That concept, even as just a chapter title, is very important and meaningful. I have a hard time putting that concept into practice myself, but as I said before, humility is one of the best practices a manager can possess. Every time we disregard someone's thought or idea without exploring or expanding on it, we continue to dull the spirit of the one who brought it to us. And it's important to have managers filled with excitement! If they have excitement, their team will have excitement by proxy.

I mentioned earlier that we were having a culture issue in the office. Justin and I had little to no respect from the team. This was in part due to the underlying management style of compassion to a fault. If you give someone an inch, they will take a mile. If you continue to give miles, they will walk all over you—not exactly the best environment to have.

Justin, again, was the only person who saw this issue coming a mile away. I mentioned at the beginning of this book that Justin's management style wasn't allowed in the office. He liked to run a tight ship with fear. This company doesn't like to manage through fear, which is absolutely fair. However, that doesn't mean you can't hold your team accountable.

In fact, our environment had very little accountability. One day, we brought the problem setter into our office and sat down. Justin told him that he was being far too much of a distraction during meetings and we needed him to take it down a notch. The setter looked Justin square in the face and simply said, "No."

Justin looked confused and borderline angry that someone would reject such a simple request. "What do you mean, no?" Justin asked.

The setter, without breaking his stare, said verbatim, "If you can't keep the attention of the class, that's on you, not me."

With the look on Justin's face, I was imagining smoke coming out of his ears. While this was incredibly out of line and disrespectful, no one would get to the point of saying something like that from nowhere.

There's something rotten in Denmark.

We had a massive issue with our office culture.

I knew the culture was the number-one issue, but I needed a foundation to begin to construct a renovated one. Considering Justin was the only one who saw our current issues coming, I wanted to see what would happen if we started instituting some of his managerial style—not to the fullest extent, of course, but enough to bring in a system of accountability while simultaneously having Justin feel more involved in the office he was supposedly meant to run.

Before I explain the culture shift, let's break down some of the issues we were having. We had approximately twenty-five setters with an "office minimum" of eight leads generated per week per person. I put office minimum in quotes because if there's no repercussions, there's no such thing as a minimum. It's just a suggestion. In fact, over half our team wasn't producing at our office minimum. There were quite a few people who showed up to meetings to hang out but never actually went out and worked. There were also some who disappeared for weeks at a time and would swing by whenever they felt like working again. It was a bit of a mess.

If we were going to incorporate some accountability, we needed to do it in a very particular way. We didn't want fear to be the forefront of our culture. We needed it to simply be an underlying reality. We weren't going to tell our team, "You need to do this or else!" We wanted everyone to understand our expectation, and when they weren't fulfilling the expectation, we would deal with them individually. Once one person experiences any form of accountability, the rest of the team will get the message.

In order to execute these ideas correctly, we went to Tom for advice. A good practice for any office is to seek advice from different departments. They may see things you're not seeing. They may have dealt with things that you haven't. Besides, everyone should be on the same team, and there's no shame in asking for direction.

Tom gave us some great advice on constructing a three-week plan for setters who were underproducing. We would sit down with them individually, ask them about their numbers, and ask them what we can do to help. If the problem is simply the number of hours worked, we would put them on a plan. We would say something along the lines of, "We need you producing eight appointments per week. Right now you're at three. We will return to this next week and we need to see some progress." If they did not make progress each week, we would have to part company.

This proved to be incredibly effective. In fact, the moment we cut ties with just one setter, the rest of the team took notice. We never mentioned it to the team. We never put any focus on it. It was simply a reality in the office. If you were underproducing, you might not be able to work here anymore. Immediately, the team began showing up to meetings on time and participating more. Quite a few of our below-average producers began increasing their production a decent amount. We then paired the new underlying reality with changing the way we talked about weekly goals.

Every Monday, we would go over weekly goals for each individual. We would ask how many appointments they wanted to generate and how many appointments they thought they could keep in a week. Then the next week we would compare their goals from the previous week to what they were actually producing. Before implementing our new system, everyone set high goals because they thought they were saying what we wanted to hear, but not very many people actually achieved them. As managers, we would let it go and continue to the next week. Of course, as we all know, the definition of insanity is doing the same thing over and over and expecting different results. So, we decided to change our approach.

Now that the team was responding to accountability, we began asking each individual why they didn't hit their goals in front of the class. We were holding them accountable for what they said they wanted to produce. We would ask what kept them from producing twelve appointments in a week. We ended up with two results from this approach.

1. Setters began completing their goals more often.
2. Setters began setting realistic goals and expanding from there.

Keep in mind, you always have to be careful with the term "realistic." There have been many times I've seen someone post a goal that they never hit or even come close to hitting. Most managers I've known, including myself, will see that and think, "Yeah, right. Just post something realistic." But remember, the name of the game is productivity. If a team member is shooting for unreasonable goals, fantastic! Your immediate response as a manager should be to ask, "How do I get this person from here to there?" Whenever we use the word "realistic," we are admitting our limitations as leaders.

While seeing a big change with more success for the setter team was incredible, can you guess where we had the greatest change?

In this process, Justin was given the opportunity to point out a structural issue and build a process in a version of his management style that showed immediate success. Justin very quickly became a whole new manager with new skills that honestly no one ever knew he possessed. His hands weren't tied anymore. He was able to demonstrate value in a very meaningful and productive way. Before, the management was afraid to give him creative control because his disposition seemed harsh or negative, but things trapped in a cage respond differently than things free in the wild.

Now we have a super positive, highly motivational Tony Robbins Justin. You can't put a price on the sheer value a manager like that brings to a team. I've always hated when managers play motivational YouTube videos to provide a fleeting sense of hype for the team. That usually only lasts about an hour. When you have someone bring you that motivation in person from such an authentic place, that hype doesn't leave you. You work, live, and breathe that environment.

Creative control is a way for people to buy in to their work. It's a way of allowing someone to grow and expand and evolve into a leader you might never have considered that person to be. Of course, it depends on their mindset as well as their environment, but the environment is the part you can help with. Is the environment you constructed suffocating their spirit? Is your environment suffocating their creativity? Are you limiting how happy and excited someone is in their position? Are you limiting their buy-in?

It's too easy for everyone to point to that person and say that they're not growing or they're not driven. You should always look to the environment first. Take some time to understand your environment and how it affects people. We're farming here, and a garden needs a variety of conditions to produce. We need to nourish and maintain it consistently or it withers.

I don't know what I would do if I didn't have any form of creative control. Of course, the moment I took this position, I may have come in like a wrecking ball. Again, I complain a lot. I require space, and honestly, the amount of space I have has allowed me to find strengths and work on skills that I never imagined I would possess. We learn through constant introduction to the unknown. If we constantly work in an environment of straight order, it might be stable, but there's nothing to learn in day after day of order, everything the same, nothing changing. There's nothing to expand on, nothing to help you grow and evolve.

The difference between when I was just a wallflower and my introduction of incentivizing behavior is night and day. Sure, the money was good when I was a wallflower, but again, money is a terrible motivator. The moment I was able to implement my ideas, I was excited! When the rest of the management team was on board, they became excited! We collaborated on new ideas that were fun and productive, and all that excitement was transferred to the setter team. I sold the setter team on my ideas because I was genuinely sold on my ideas. It doesn't get any better than that!

In fact, the immediate excitement Justin and I produced at that time made us rock stars in the company. People wanted to know what we were doing. Offices wanted to know how we were accomplishing anything. And we were just skimming the surface of what could really be accomplished. This was just one small aspect of a much larger culture issue that we were dealing with, but we were on to something.

A couple weeks later, I was in a management meeting with all offices in the state, and I had quite a few managers approach me to ask about what I was doing. One mentioned that they felt like I came in and started implementing anti-corporate policies and was wondering how I was able to get away with it. I asked that person what type of ideas they had been playing around with and testing. I was asking about their level of creative control. They responded, "I didn't know we could do anything like that. I thought we were just filling a position." How excited about your work can you possibly be if you believe you are just filling a position?

Let your management team thrive. Let go of your chokehold on the office. Allow your team to work with creative control and see just how incredible and diverse their ideas, structures, and procedures can really be. Allow them to buy in fully and enjoy watching them transform from mere managers to great leaders.

Chapter 5:

The Perception of Opportunity

A very real and unfortunate truth is that most people are motivated by a fear of loss rather than a desire to gain. There are very few people in this world who will run as fast as they can in order to attain a gold medal. For every person who will, there are millions who will run as fast as they can only in the event they are being chased down by a German Shepard. It sounds funny if we think about that specific scenario, but it is true in most aspects of life. Who is really, actually putting their all into developing any certain skill or set of skills that will move them toward the top of their field? Or even toward the top of their own social circles?

This, again, is an issue that we have with internal resistance. It is so much easier to swerve toward immediate gratification, and in America specifically, immediate gratification is far too easy to find. To overcome this tendency really demands some self-control.

Everything boils down to mindset. Sometimes we just need to make a switch in our head that reprioritizes what's important in our lives. Generally, we grow up dreamers. We aspire to be something special and great, always imagining ourselves being at the very top. However, once it comes down to personal production, drive, and discipline, we slow down. We drink more. We smoke more. We work less and produce less when we are technically working. We eat out more. We work out less. Resistance simply amplifies these behaviors. This insidious force turns us to our vices at every opportunity. It promotes the self-medicating numbness that allows us to coast in our lives. That's our "comfort zone." We call it a comfort zone, but there's really nothing comfortable about it. We never thought we were going to set up shop and waste away some of our most capable years. In the grand scheme of things, no one wants to be in the comfort zone. Every time we're sitting at home watching *Family Guy* reruns and eating half a pizza, we think, "Man I really could use some more money" or "I wish I could afford a house" or "I wish I had the body I used to have" or "I wish I had a better relationship with my parents" or "I wish I had friends with interesting hobbies."

Is this wish time now? How long does this last?

Apparently, wish time is a state of being. The truth is that long-term growth requires discipline. Every time that we make a choice in favor of immediate gratification, we are only prolonging our long-term growth and success.

How many years ago did you graduate high school? Think about what you wanted then. You planned to buy a house fairly quickly. You found a temporary job until you could get started on your career. Or maybe the temp job offered the career you wanted but you haven't put in the time and effort to move up the ladder. You say it's temporary, but how many years has it been? How many years are you going to stay in your comfort zone and prolong the start of your life?

I once dated a girl who had a fantastic habit. Whenever she was bored, she never said, "I'm bored." Instead, she said, "I'm boring." That is a great trick to change your mindset. If you constantly tell yourself "I'm boring" when you have nothing to do, you will find something to do. No one wants to admit they're boring.

Grant Cardone says that "success is a responsibility." I couldn't agree more. I need to get that tattooed on my forehead so that when I look in the mirror, I start my day with every action pointing toward success. That's how mindset works. There's a huge difference in how you work and present yourself in the real world depending on how you think. If you think you want to be successful, or if you think that success is simply your destination, those thoughts won't drive you the same way as thinking it is your responsibility to be successful.

Accountability is motivation by fear of loss. No one wants to lose their job or be in trouble. That's why when you implement a structure based on accountability, you will find it affects most people. If a worker is motivated by success, they won't even bother with external accountability. They will be far above the realm necessary for it because they have strong internal accountability. That's powerful.

When it comes to understanding a path to success, I believe most people imagine it represented by a diagonal line. The more you work, the further up the line of success you go. Clearly, that's not accurate. If it were, everyone would be successful. Everyone would see immediate results from their work and continue to produce. I understand success as a horizontal line with a sharp curve.

We start far away from the curve, and the more work we put in, the closer we move toward the curve. That means we're not seeing success until we eventually hit the curve and begin to move up. Considering it takes some time and effort to reach the curve, people tend to quit or burn out because they're not seeing the results quickly enough. In a way, it's a lot like working out. If you work out for a few months and lose a few pounds, you're not going to be ripped. You have to make working out part of your lifestyle in order to see the real success of being in shape. If it is part of your lifestyle and you're consistently doing it, you will reach the curve. That's what falling in love with the process is all about—sticking it out consistently long enough to reach the curve.

Price's law (also known as the square root law) was created by Derek J. de Solla Price. This law pertains to the production output in various fields or environments. Price found that within career environments, the square root of the workers involved in a collaborative field did approximately half of all the work. This means that if twenty-five authors contribute one hundred papers, fifty of those papers come from only five of those authors. The other fifty papers come from the other twenty authors collectively. That's an interesting statistic. Think about it. If there are one hundred workers, it means only ten of them will do half the work. What are those other guys doing?

This law was also reflected in our office. When we had twenty-five setters, only about five of them were doing half the work.

Price's law can then be layered over the Pareto distribution. The Pareto distribution (also known as the 80/20 rule) was originally applied to wealth distribution. Vilfredo Pareto stated that 80 percent of the wealth belonged to 20 percent of the population. This can also be applied to productivity. To be successful, you want to be part of the square root that does the extra work and earns the extra wealth. If success is a horizontal line with a sharp curve, there is quite a lot of work to be done before seeing the first sign of success. Is this why people give up so quickly? At some point, you become so productive that the moment you get traction on that curve, there's almost no stopping you. But it's getting to that point that is the hardest part. It's putting in the grind. It's putting in the blood, sweat, and tears while seeing little results.

If you don't make the necessary adjustments to consistently move toward success, your subconscious autopilot will only keep you well enough to survive. If you fear losing your job, you will work just enough extra to keep it. If you fear losing your house, you will find the money to keep yourself off the streets. Is that really how we want to live though? Just on the edge of complete failure? That seems to be where most of us are—one month away from being on the streets. It's sad to think that's where we set up shop for so long.

One time I was walking through a park with a friend. There was a cement walkway that snaked its way around the park. My friend and I were glued to our phone screens, walking on the cement, when all of a sudden, a homeless man on a bike ran right into my friend just next to me! Of course, we were angry and surprised. The homeless man, now off his bike, reached into his backpack and brandished a hammer in response to our exclamations. This was far more trouble than we wanted. We backed up, using our phones to call the police. He came at us, distraught and swinging. My friend told him, "I'm calling the police, man! I don't know what your problem is."

The homeless man stood still, stared at us, pointed the hammer at us, and said, "You all are just one paycheck away from being where I am."

This is a true story. And was he wrong? It seems that most people tend to keep themselves on a paycheck-to-paycheck level of living even when opportunity is right in front of them. So, how do we move people up the curve? Is it possible to create an office with a better distribution ratio than Price's law? I sure would like to think so.

Let's start by thinking about the most basic form of motivation in a workplace. That would have to be pay, but what exactly is pay? I already believe that money is a terrible motivator, but it is an important motivator. With how poorly our team was producing, clearly pay isn't enough of a motivator for everyone. So what do people work toward in a door-to-door environment? Well, some people like the idea of moving up. I know I do. In fact, personally, I took a pay cut in order to move into management. Some people really like to parade around as well.

So, how can we use certain office aspects to increase motivation?

People are compensated in different ways, as well as motivated differently. Personally, I use three methods of compensation in my management. Those three methods of compensation are money, status, and the perception of opportunity. I say *perception* because if someone can't see opportunity, they won't move toward it. We have to make the opportunity incredibly visible to everyone. Unfortunately, when people finally get an opportunity or promotion, they generally tend to rest easy instead of working harder to make the most of it.

Say your office pays fairly well, but your workers as a whole aren't working that hard. If you throw more money at them, you may get a few more to work harder, but the majority will work less because they made more money with less work. Again, what *should* work isn't always what *does* work. A lot of people have a terrible concept of money, which means you may have to change the form of compensation.

A great example of this actually happened before I became a manager. As I explained earlier, Asia and Justin created an office structure that included the role of a "team lead"—four individuals who were highly productive. The team leads were basically captains, and the rest of the office was split into teams. Those captains would invite their teams out on the doors and motivate them as peers, which, at first, turned out to be very effective. Those team leads were compensated with a cut of their team's production. Sounds good so far.

At some point after this new structure was implemented, everyone started working less, including those who were normally incredibly consistent. The spirit in the office became dull, and there wasn't much motivation. There was extra money being thrown around in an attempt to spark something, but it just wasn't doing the trick.

Asia called me one day to ask if I had noticed anything that could help her. I explained my concept of compensation. Then I asked if the four team leads were working harder than their peers. They weren't. In fact, because the team lead position was a tenured position, those four individuals became comfortable with the cut they were making from their team and they began to work *less* than the rest of their team.

How would you feel if the person supposedly leading you is staying home making money off of your work? That has to be one of the most disincentivizing things I can imagine. It's not that the setters were being paid less. In fact, they get paid well. This was a problem with tenure that also applies to nepotism. The team lead position represented status. It showed their peers they were at the top of the class. If a position like that is locked up and no one can work to earn it, people lose any perception of opportunity at the company. They have no sense of direction and nowhere to go. Even if they technically have opportunity, perception is everything. The office was lacking two important forms of compensation.

Luckily for me, Asia made immediate changes. Of course, me not being a manager at the time, this didn't affect me one bit; however, I love to see whether my ideas work.

Asia switched up the team lead position to rotate every two weeks. The four setters with the highest production (measured in in appointments held) got to be a team lead and were given a chance to demonstrate leadership. We saw a change overnight. People began working twice as hard because now there was a status position they could earn. That meant something! There was something to earn that would validate their hard work and determination, which is a very important tool to use.

When there is a free-flowing form of meritocracy in an office, there is a very positive shift on a subconscious level. The subconscious level is incredibly overlooked and undervalued. Of course, my goal here is to explain how it is of the utmost importance.

In fact, let's go back to something I said earlier: "You get out what you put in." In a setup where a few people are constantly rewarded with status and pay because they were good at one time (tenure), does that give off the perception of getting out what you put in? Or are you relaying to your team that to get somewhere, it's all about who you know and how long you stay? The message you are sending by constantly rewarding the few people with the longest tenure is that those people worked their way up there, and now they can rest easy. If that's the message you're sending, why would anyone want to work hard? Where's the motivation? Imagine the confusion that ensues when you tell a recruit that they get out of this job what they put into it. When that recruit comes in and sees the structures locked up, they're going to immediately lose trust in the leadership of the company. What you say and what you practice are two completely different things. I really need you, as a reader, to understand how important the psychology of this is.

Again, let's go back to something I mentioned before. When an office has a statement, objective, or promise, that idea has to echo throughout the environment. We have to create an environment that makes those statements, objectives, and promises an actual reality and possibility. We need to untangle the mess of cords that confuses the subconscious and reveal a clear ethos that is both stated and practiced. When that path is cleared, one of the most valuable forms of compensation will be realized by everyone on the team: the perception of opportunity.

Let's even take this idea from the setter side to the closer side. Say you manage a sales team. Do you give the most leads or the best leads to the person who has been with you the longest? Do you give them to the person who is your closest friend? Do you have a couple people who always receive the best and most leads because that's the way things have always been done in your office? Isn't your job to build people up? Isn't your job to make sure everyone is progressing and becoming better? If you have your setup locked up like that, where is the motivation for anyone to get better? I'm not even just talking about the people who want to be at the top; I'm talking about the ones already there. If you're constantly being handed easy leads, are you developing as a salesperson? If you constantly have three to four leads a day, are you going to treat them all as if you only had one for the day? The tenured people eventually get spoiled and jaded and only go after the low-hanging fruit while the rest of the team becomes disincentivized to try any harder. What's the point? There's no room for growth here.

That kind of environment will only bring down the production of the tenured team members through complacency while simultaneously bringing down the production of the rest of the team by wearing down their spirit. You may think you have the right people in the right places, and let's say you do. If they are indeed the best salespeople, won't they stay at the top with a meritocracy system as well? It's poor logic to think you need to protect your top producers.

In reality, if you have a system based on meritocracy (like your office promise may say), you will have your top producers working harder to protect their top spot—always on their toes and showing why they were at the top in the first place. You will also have the rest of the team working harder because they can *see* the opportunity and the path forward. You might find that someone rises up and overtakes all the tenured people. That's when you know you made the right choice.

Ultimately, with a meritocracy system, you will greatly increase your office production compared to a tenured system. It's more psychologically sound. It incentivizes excellence and work ethic. People need to be able to see the path forward. People need to understand that there is a path forward. Take a look at your structures. Take a look at the statements you make. Do they line up? If you put yourself in your workers' position, do you see a way forward?

In fact, let's move this away from a moral or psychological argument. Let's take a look at the opportunity cost of not using a meritocracy system. Now we're talking about numbers, right? A lot of people read books looking for ways to increase their pay, so let's talk about that.

Opportunity cost is the amount you could have made or could be making if you had taken the correct action or implemented the correct structure or idea. We'll use easy math here. Say the product at your company brings in $1,000 of profit for every sale. You're currently using a tenure system for your team, and it seems to be running well. Your office is bringing in approximately $6,000 a day in profit. Not bad. Say you're reading this and you just don't agree with the meritocracy system of shifting people around based on performance. Maybe you don't have the heart to take leads away from your friends. Three months go by and your office is plugging along and still making approximately $6,000 a day. Well, offices aren't meant to be stagnant. Offices are meant to rapidly increase production over time. Why are you okay with the stagnation? Your bosses sure aren't. They're checking the stat sheets and seeing zero growth over three months. Now they're telling you that you need to find a way to increase production. You may come down on your team and tell them to work harder. Again, that doesn't work so well. You may think about hiring new employees but you have all the appointments covered. Now that you have nothing left to try, you introduce the meritocracy method. You may have some pushback from your employees at first, but really quickly you notice they're working differently. They're taking more time with their clients. They're not cutting corners or skipping steps. You find that a salesperson you didn't believe in is now closing at a high level, and your office production increases by 20 percent!

Let's break that percentage down. Your product brings in $1,000 per sale. You were averaging $6,000 per day. So, on average, your team brings in six sales per day. Your company runs six days per week, so that's thirty-six sales per week at $36,000 of profit per week. That is $144,000 per month. A 20 percent increase means that you are now averaging 7.2 sales per day. That is $7,200 on average per day. That is $43,200 per week. Which brings you to $172,800 per month. That is $28,800 more per month! Fantastic!

Well, wait a minute. Your office was stagnant for three months. Seeing the increase in measurable results, you wonder, what if you had started this system three months prior? That is where opportunity cost comes in. Because you decided to wait before trying a good idea, your office missed out on a total of $86,400 over a three-month span! That's over half a month's worth of revenue compared to what you were previously bringing in! If you had tried the new idea first, your bosses wouldn't have come down on you, and you would've looked like a rock star. And what was it for? You didn't want to let down your friends? Trust me, they're happier now. They're working smarter, selling more, and making more money!

Now that we've looked at both the setter side and sales side, let's take a step back and look at the structure from top to bottom. You may think those two sides are completely different teams. They don't have anything to do with each other. Don't mix your chocolate with my peanut butter! It's true that they are two separate teams, but they are very much connected on many levels. The most important level of connection is that they're part of the same office! You don't just disregard teams in your office. You want them to mingle.

Any office is an interconnected machine, and the way you have your systems set up with one team will affect the rest. For example, let's say a decent number of setters come into our company with the intention of one day becoming a closer. Now, if our team lead position is locked up on the setter side, will they feel there is any upward mobility? It sure wouldn't feel that way to me. But if the team lead position is available and you acquired that as a new setter, you might start seeing opportunity more clearly and may begin to think about management or moving to the sales side.

But then what if the sales side is locked up? Do you think that if the setters notice that the sales side is locked up it might impair their perception of opportunity? Do you think that, based on the structures at the top, the people at the entry level may never work hard enough to reach the top because they can't see the opportunity? Is it their fault that they can't see it?

If the lack of perception of opportunity is due to the environment, we create the environment. That's on us. We are holding our team back whether we realize it or not. You may think that is a result of a weak mindset, but not everyone is on the same level. For people to see a way forward, we need to meet them on their level and lead them to the next. We need to facilitate an environment that reciprocates.

In fact, let me expand on that idea a bit further. As leaders, we have to meet our team at the level that they are at. There is a process of self-improvement that must take place—in all aspects of life, including work, relationships, health, hobbies, families, etc. The difference between leaders and workers is that leaders are simply further along in the same process. It takes some people longer to get there, but it is the same process. With this concept in mind, everyone has the capacity to do anything. My team has the same capacity to lead as I do. They have the same capacity to lead as my bosses. They are simply not as far along in the process. Perhaps some of the concepts and opportunities we know simply aren't understood by your team yet because they haven't come far enough in the process to begin to perceive those opportunities. It's our job as leaders to meet them where they are in the process and help lead them in a forward direction. This can take time;

however, if you care about the growth of your team and keep at it, eventually they will begin to perceive the opportunities.

If we don't take the time to help our team recognize their potential, how will they move in an upward direction? What about if there is no sense of meritocracy? What about upward mobility in terms of management? Do you think promoting your friends might impair the perception of opportunity for other strong candidates and up-and-comers? Do you think promoting your friends might incentivize playing the game instead of trusting the process? Do you want members of your team to play the game? Do you want them to get close to you because they know if they're your buddy, that's their best chance of getting ahead? Do you enjoy being used?

Again, think of the office environment like a machine. Everything is interconnected. Gears are turning. The setters feed the sales side. We're shoveling cash into the furnace when all of a sudden everything slows down. That's strange. It's only running at half capacity. The natural inclination is to shovel more cash in faster thinking this will get it back on track—but it doesn't. Then we stand back scratching our heads because it never occurred to us that we have three different types of fuel: cash, status, and perception of opportunity! At this point, it's time to try the other fuels and see how they work out.

You may also run a diagnostic and realize that a gear is stuck. Well, if the office is a machine and one gear is stuck, does that not affect the entire machine? Maybe there is just one small aspect of the workplace where we can make a minor adjustment to get the whole office moving again at maximum capacity! We need to be incredibly conscious of the interconnection of everything in an office environment.

I know I've been talking about the perception of opportunity a lot in this chapter. (I mean, it is the title after all.) But aside from the work environment, do you think perception of opportunity may have something to with people's normal habits in life? Do you think that maybe someone never became a famous actress because they simply couldn't see the path to get there? Maybe someone always wanted to open a restaurant. They dreamed about being the owner of some hit new eatery, but dreams are just dreams, right?

I have to admit, I've wanted to write a book since I was in high school. I thought about it continuously throughout my life; however, I always thought I didn't have the skills. I didn't have enough source materials. I didn't know if anyone would want to read about my ideas. I didn't know what platforms to use. Where is the path?

> I had to get to a personal level of production where I finally understood how unproductive the majority of people are, and I realized the people who have their own books are simply the ones who sat down to write them.

Now my perception of opportunity is bigger because my vision is greater, although not everyone has reached this level. It's our job as leaders to show our teams the path forward. More importantly, it's our job to construct and maintain an environment that allows for a path forward to be seen.

Perception is everything.

Chapter 6

Be Proactive, Not Reactive

D o you feel overwhelmed? Do you find yourself trying to ignite a spark with your team but no one has bought in? You can't spend too much time barking up that tree considering you have to get ahead on your own numbers, but you also need to come up with a new program for this month. It was supposed to be done last week, but there have been too many fires to put out. You want to get started on training someone to move up, but you've been holding off until you correct some problem individuals in the office. Some great workers leave suddenly. Your office has another bad day, so you decide to make a last-minute incentive to pay whoever gets the most production before close of business for the day. The results-based incentives then disincentivize the rest of the team. Now you're paying more to work against your goals and it feels like you're sinking in quicksand. You may not have even realized you were in quicksand at first, but the process starts super slowly and gradually becomes relentless. You try to deal with things as they come, but sometimes too much comes at once and you become stuck. You have no direction—and no way out.

We've all been there. Instead of dealing with problems as they arise, it is much more beneficial—not to mention manageable—to get ahead of issues before they come up. Before a situation arises, it's incredibly important to forecast and plan. If you notice any trends, foresee any upcoming issues, or understand seasonal changes, you must create protocols to put in place *before* those things occur. If you have to react to issues as they come, situations become much more difficult to salvage and you run the risk of looking desperate or incompetent.

If you can navigate foreseeable changes with smooth transitions, you are successfully getting ahead of the game. You might find yourself having to make reactionary decisions every once in a while, but now maybe only a day will get away from you. However, if you find yourself constantly making reactionary decisions, that's the whole industry getting away from you.

A reactionary decision looks a lot like the following scenario. Again, I'm going to use a door-to-door example since that's my industry. Let's say that your team just isn't producing one day. It's far below the daily standard, and you're afraid you may get a call from upper management. If you were to put out a last-minute incentive to pay a little extra for the last few hours of the night, who is really going to get out on the streets for just the last couple hours? Not many people. You're going to maybe end up with slightly more production, but the worst outcome is that when the team sees low production after the reactionary incentive, they will view management as being desperate. Also, if the team doesn't reach that particular incentive goal, they will be less likely to work the next day. Now you have lost a day and a half and paid more for net negative appointments.

Whenever an instance like that occurs, I always let the night play out and then salvage the bad day by posting a fun incentive the next day. The team feels as though it was planned and considering they basically took one day off, they are more likely to work harder the next day, greatly increasing your production. Just understanding the way your team will perceive your actions helps you make better decisions when issues arise.

Being proactive with incentives in general is a great habit. Personally, I like to take some time each month to brainstorm with my team and think about the issues we want to get ahead of in the upcoming months. Of course, back in Chapter 3, we talked about our "It's not late, it's just dark" incentive, where we got ahead of the winter months when it would be dark around 5 p.m. by getting our team to work in the dark during the fall months. Just getting the team accustomed to working in the dark in general made it a super easy transition for the rest of the year.

Most home improvement or installation companies slow down drastically during the last six weeks of the year. It's dark, it's cold, and it's raining or snowing. It's the holidays. There are a lot of excuses we make as managers during this time, and I have seen managers give in to this as a reality. When a manager gives in to an idea being a reality, they make it a reality—but it doesn't have to be. Your holiday season can be as big as your vision is. If you have a small, defeated, or myopic vision, that's what your outcome will be. But if you have a dominant and productive vision, you won't even slow down. You can get your team to produce great numbers during this time of year. You may just have to get a little creative and fun. I like to make team incentives during the holiday season instead of individual incentives. If you have a prize that's good enough and make the team reliant on each other, you will encourage members of the team to continue to work just so they won't let their teammates down. It's equally, if not more, important for you as a manager to be out in the field suffering in the rain with them. Be the example they need, especially during the difficult months.

Get ahead of anything you can. If it's going to be raining for a week or two, look at that and think about how to get ahead of it. If elections are happening and half the homeowners are furious, think about what angles and words we are going to use. If crazy or negative news that even somewhat pertains to the industry is in the mainstream, we need to construct talk tracks and role-play how to overcome that with our team. You might think that everyone will use these instances to take a break or you don't want to overwhelm them. While I never want to overwhelm my team, the truth is that by getting ahead and implementing these strategies, we are simply adding more tools to our teams' toolboxes. Each individual will be much better at their job and more likely to succeed in any circumstance. That's empowering a team!

It's always good to be proactive with lessons and training. This is actually an area in which I personally haven't done the best. Normally my training would focus on any current weaknesses in our team. This, of course, is important; however, if we only teach things that we are currently struggling with, we forget to teach many other aspects of the job and will constantly have new issues arise. Say, for instance, your focus is on getting families to keep their appointments. We may spend a lot of time training people how to confirm appointments or how to set expectations. Then in the next meeting we may talk about the best ways to follow up. We may spend a week or two on one aspect but then the teams start cutting corners and having trouble with the basics. Because they're basics, we generally think everyone has mastered those aspects; however, all salespeople will cut corners or skip steps from time to time, resulting in them becoming less productive, and they won't even recognize the issue. If we constantly went back to the basics while we also taught the current issue, this might not come up as an issue in the future. Teams need to review all aspects of the job regularly. It's incredibly valuable to your team to continuously have their minds refreshed when it comes to systems, strategies, and protocols.

I'm currently working on a system where I put everything we can teach into categories. I don't believe you need a lot of categories, maybe two or three. For my team, I'm using the following categories: basic training, intermediate training, advanced training, and current issues. I brainstorm everything we teach with my management team and then assign each thing a categories. During each meeting, we can talk about one thing from each category and have them rotate. That way, we have a good lesson for everyone in the room regardless of how far along they are, we cover the current issues in the office, and we constantly get ahead of issues that may arise in the future.

Promotions are also something we can be proactive about. I wouldn't necessarily say promote quickly but have people on track learning the next job so they are ready when an opening presents itself. In my company, there are two directions in which you can be promoted. People can move into selling deals or they can move into management.

If someone comes in as a setter and is incredibly dedicated, producing massive numbers consistently for a long period of time, naturally you want to give them the option of moving to the next position. Unfortunately, many companies see someone excelling and try as hard as they can to keep that individual in their current position. If you don't give that individual the option to move up, no one on the team will see the path forward. There will be no perception of opportunity, and you run the risk of losing that driven individual. If you then promote someone who is doing less than that individual, you are teaching your team to aim for average. It's generally better to do what's best for the team instead what achieves only short-term gains. Any office is an infinite game, and it should be about personal growth as well as office growth.

If you find that your team is producing at a level where other departments can't keep up with the sheer volume, that's when you need to promote. Again, you may not want to promote immediately but at least put people on the path. Give a couple people some metrics to hit over time in order to get there. They will be excited about the opportunity. A rite of passage like this can be used as a great coaching tool. There have been times I've been quick to promote and those individuals rest easy once they get there. Technically, they should be working harder, but we made it easy, so they took it easy. If you have a rite of passage that requires high production to get to the next level, you are setting the expectation for that level of production. When you help build them up to that level and then move them over, it becomes a lot more natural.

The reason you want to act fast when you run into this situation is because the meritocracy structure you built for the sales team no longer exists if you're producing more than what they can run. If every salesperson has their days booked up consistently, there is no reason for them to try their best to earn more appointments or status. People will strive to succeed during famine just to survive. Times of plenty are when we tend to become complacent, cut corners, and skip steps. We become jaded and only look for the low-hanging fruit. We want to add to their team to create balance. The ones who take care of their appointments will be filled up, the ones that don't, won't. Feast, as opposed to famine, is not just a sign that your office is doing well; it's also a sign that your teams are out of balance. Get ahead of that before the closer team starts wasting their appointments.

In a way, it's best to manufacture famine during a feast. If you have enough salespeople to fill up the day for some, halfway for others, and just one appointment for others, that's when your sales team is going to shine. Maybe they were all feasting with ten salespeople, but with twenty? You can spread out the feast to build a structure that has closers chasing status, opportunity, and/ or money.

Now let's apply this to management. When it comes to upward mobility into management, is it better to wait to train someone until a position has opened up? Or is it better to have a few good candidates who learn from you so you have a group of capable people to choose from? Different companies definitely see it differently, and many managers don't like to teach their position to the people below them out of fear of being replaced. I believe that teaching a few people how to do your job both mechanically and theoretically is a positive thing. It shows that you are a proactive person. If for some reason you can't make a meeting, someone can step in. If you get promoted, you already have candidates ready to take your old spot. You will earn the trust of your team, and those candidates will be loyal to you. As an added bonus, while you are running your team, these candidates will become better leaders and provide better help to the team.

I don't believe we should ever let fear be a deciding factor in whether we do something. If most managers fear being replaced, mentoring candidates will show strength. If demoting someone makes you fear not having a large enough team, doing so will punctuate importance to your team. If promoting someone makes you fear losing production, that person definitely deserves a promotion and doing so will show their peers the opportunity that comes with strong production, and someone will fill the void that person left.

It's always good to be proactive with goals as well. Having an objective to fight toward is incredibly important for a team. If you have a target to rally behind, your team will buy in to the hype alone of something greater than just working a job. They are part of a team, a camaraderie, a family, a tribe—and you are hunting a big game. The thrill of the hunt is an incredible driving force that can last months, and the sense of accomplishment from completing the objective can be otherworldly. However, once the accomplishment is over, the team will revert back to normal work if the goal is not replaced. If you are intending to grow and scale your office, it's important to have the next goal on deck for when you complete the first.

I mentioned before that we used to chant "Road to 200" throughout the year, aiming at the goal of having 200 new contracts written in one month. We managed to get there, which was a major accomplishment for us and the company. The mistake that we made is that we never replaced that goal. After we hit the 200 contracts, everyone went back to normal, and we consistently wrote less than 200 each month thereafter. In fact, we let four months pass before we instituted "Road to 250." Four months is far too much time to let slip away. We showed a pinnacle of production, and then we took a four-month siesta.

The goal for my team is no longer competitive. There is no other office in the company that can compete on our level right now, so I've been entirely focused on dominating the area in which we work. We have a very large team that works every day. I don't want any other solar company find money in the area we work. I am looking to straight suffocate the local market. Because I have taken to this way of thinking, my team has also taken to this way of thinking. At the same time, because it's fun, Justin decided to introduce a goal on top of that for our singular office in Virginia to produce more than all the offices in the entire state of Texas! This sounds crazy considering we're a solar company and Texas has far more opportunity than Virginia; however, at the moment I'm writing this, our office has more production than all our offices in the state of Texas. Domination is all about mindset, and your office can only grow as big as the vision you cast.

A lack of being proactive shows insecurity. Insecurity can keep you from taking an action for fear of making a mistake or from mentoring your team for fear of losing your job. Insecurity can also keep you from taking risks for fear of damaging your ego if those risks don't pan out. Not everything is going to work, but the more initiative you take, the faster you will get through the process. The more you learn to flesh ideas out on your own, the more stable you become as a leader.

I recently read a book by Carol Dweck called *Mindset*. This book focuses on what she considers "fixed" and "growth" mindsets. A fixed mindset, as she describes it, is a mindset driven by ego. The main downfall of ego is that it has a disposition to avoid attempting tasks, processes, and concepts that are seemingly difficult or alien. You avoid these things because you don't want to show weakness or failure. That would damage your ego. Well, they say if you fail to plan, you plan to fail, and if you're reluctant to progress through the introduction of the unknown, there is no growth to be had.

This mindset is apparently a normal obstacle for the naturally talented. If someone is constantly praised for their talent, they will rely on their talent instead of hard work and progression. Talent, of course, needs to be developed further. Many people become managers because of their natural abilities. As a manager, you may pigeonhole yourself into certain areas in which you thrive because you don't want to show how underdeveloped your understanding is in other areas.

One of my favorite lines from Jordan Peterson's *12 Rules for Life* is: "Winning at everything might only mean that you're not doing anything new or difficult. You might be winning but you're not growing, and growing might be the most important form of winning. Should victory in the present always take precedence over trajectory across time?"

Which game are you playing? Victory in the present? Doing the same things, taking the same actions time after time because you enjoy the victory? That's a fixed mindset game. Trajectory across time is the infinite game. If there were two offices, one thrilled with its small victories and the other set on growth and expansion over time, which do you think would come out on top? Isn't it fair to say that if you're always coming out on top of the same victories replayed again and again, there's nowhere to go but down? If your office buys in to traversing the chaos and becoming 1 percent better every day, it's a consistent climb that theoretically never ends. That's working with a growth mindset.

A growth mindset, as defined in *Mindset*, is to understand that it's not about the outcome; it's about the process. It's not about the destination; it's about the journey. It's not about the answer; it's about the steps taken to get there. A growth mindset does not shy away from taking action; it thrives in the experience. It learns from it. It understands that mistakes must be made to progress understanding toward being a more complete individual and leader.

A growth mindset does not fear competition, for if you are consistently growing, who will catch you? When you understand this, the act of mentoring a capable person will never threaten you. You will strive to bring them up with you, and they will respect you for it. If you embrace a growth mindset, you will naturally become more active, as well as proactive, in your leadership.

The bottom line in all things is: be proactive, not reactive.

Chapter 7:

Door-to-Door Dogma

'm generally a sucker for psychology. Philosophy, on the other hand, I've always regarded as cheap. That may not be a fair summation of the history of philosophy considering we've mapped incredible methods to pursue understanding; however, I view philosophy as a doorway to pass through early in life so that you can more quickly navigate concepts throughout life. I wouldn't personally devote a significant portion of life to contemplating it, let alone revising or expanding it.

That being said, I do owe credit for my learning methods to my early studies and understanding of Georg Hegel. Hegel was a philosopher who lived during the turn of the nineteenth century and developed a dialectic geared toward the evolution of ideas and concepts. In what's known today as Hegelian dialectic, Hegel used a three-value model that follows the path of abstract, negative, and concrete. His idea of abstract replaces the idea of thesis. A thesis is normally the starting point in discovery and is first presented to discuss or flesh out an idea. The word "thesis," however, doesn't imply inherent, internal flaws. Therefore, he opted to use the word "abstract," which naturally implies lack of structure and cohesion.

With this model, you begin with the understanding that every idea, concept, or structure is, at least at first, inherently abstract. The abstract has to go through a process of "negative" in order to find flaws. The process of negative is, as the name implies, like poking holes in an idea. At least, that's how you would see it through the lens of ego. However, if you are looking for understanding, it's simply ironing the flaws out of a concept. Once the flaws are ironed out, what was once abstract can now be considered "concrete."

Unfortunately, in this day and age, ego is so prevalent that most forms of disagreement can easily be seen as an attack. Even more unfortunate is that our society manufactures ego where it's not warranted. Though, even if it is, Ryan Holiday is right to say that the ego is the enemy.

In arguments today, everyone has answers already loaded. We are not listening to each other. We are not listening for understanding. We are listening to respond. We are just waiting to drop a line, and whoever has the last word is "right"—at least in their own eyes. That seems to be the point—to show that you're right. No one benefits. In most debates, the point is generally a display of skill. If someone can debate better, they merely show that they have a sharp intellect and "win." Why are arguments and debate seldom used to find truth or understanding? From my understanding, I would attribute that to ego. That's where Hegelian dialectic shines. It's a method that only functions correctly in the absence of ego. It is there to evolve the quality of understanding. In fact, a key principle of Hegelian dialectic is the transition of quantity to quality.

Now, something might be considered quality or "concrete," but personally I don't like to think of anything as being perfect. I believe that no matter how fleshed out a concept or idea or structure is, there will always be flaws or room for improvement. At the very least, concepts, ideas, and structures need to change over time as the environment does.

I have used this method of learning for my own ideas, as well as to help understand the ideas of others. This, unfortunately, can make people upset because when I hear about structures that are in place, I go through the negative process with the person who made them. This can easily be misconstrued as me "poking holes" or discrediting someone else's ideas; however, I go through this process so I can better understand the structure and commit it to memory.

Using this lens, I have taken a hard look at the industry in which I work. I have found that the standards and metrics, as well as the celebration of certain behaviors, in the door-to-door industry are either flawed, incomplete, underdeveloped, or even harmful to offices. To be fair, the industry standards were tried-and-true for decades, but I've never been one to fall in line with "that's how it's always been done." The only constant is change, and as the times change, so must the processes. In fact, at this point, it is increasingly clear that the industry's standard metrics are shortsighted. This is the part of the book where I aim to iron out these ideas and concepts with the goal of constructing an office environment that will empower people, as well as raise the ceiling of what is actually possible.

"Work smarter, not harder"—we have all heard this line fairly often no matter what office or industry. It's a true enough statement, though any office I've ever worked in says it and then tells everyone to work harder. Personally, I'm a workaholic. Work is about all I do, and I'm not too good with the whole work–life balance thing, but I do try to work smarter any way I can. Generally, to me, "working smart" means that work is put toward the high-priority goal. Having a system of priorities or values is imperative if you are trying to have a productive office.

Recently, I was wrestling with the methods of prioritization within my own company. Currently, Justin and I run the most productive setter team in the country for our company. We have a super high retention rate for new employees, and we are easily the most consistent office. The funny thing about that is you wouldn't know it if you ever listened to our company-wide management videoconferences. If there is a manager who has incredibly high personal stats (since we can produce on the doors just like a setter), that will always be the person the company praises, regardless of the production of their office. Don't get me wrong, it is incredibly impressive that someone can manage a team and outproduce them at the same time; however, very important tasks fall by the wayside when that happens.

I had been prodded here and there about picking up my own personal production. Well, if there was one manager in this company who would have to, it would definitely be me. My stats are nearly nonexistent. But there was a reason for that, and it blew me away that my personal stats were a high priority. I spent a lot of time trying to understand why. This didn't make any sense to me, and it frustrated me because no matter how many times I went back to a system of priorities and tried to place it higher, it was always near the bottom of my list. I couldn't justify doing what was being asked of me through my process.

And here is my process.

First, I ask what the goal of the company is. To sell solar? To be impressive? To be well-known? Well, the goal of any company is to make money. It's that simple. And in order for the company to make money, each individual office's main focus needs to be productivity. So then office productivity is my goal, and I must create a system of prioritization with the goal of productivity. Well how many facets of an office are there? For an office to be productive, you need workers. The biggest drawback of nearly every sales office is that it's a revolving door. That means it needs strong training and good culture. Some workers fall behind and everyone needs to improve, so we need behavioral incentives that add new tools to everyone's toolboxes. We then need to brainstorm and develop ideas. As managers, we are forever students. We need to constantly be reading and listening to podcasts to progress and become the right managers to lead our team into new phases. We need to have large office goals as well as coach individual goals for our team members. We need to hold people accountable and spend time getting to know our team members so that we can understand how to help and motivate individuals.

If I lay everything out from top to bottom to prioritize my time, it looks like this:

1. Maintain Culture
2. Train New Employees
3. Develop Existing Employees
4. Recruitment
5. Office and Individual Goals
6. Reading/Podcasts
7. Research and Development
8. Scalability
9. Team Relationship Building
10. Personal Stats

With this method of prioritization, I start each day with number one: Is there anything I can do today that will help benefit or reinforce our culture? If there is, that will be what I focus on first. Then, are there new employees who need training? If so, that's my next focus, and so on.

Of course, some of these numbers are interchangeable, and I could probably move personal stats up to number eight. I can't, however, justify personal stats being anywhere near the top of my radar.

Going back to the ask that I increase my personal stats, why can't I understand it? Is there something I'm missing here? How does my personal stats contribute on a large scale toward the goal?

Leading from the front is not just a management style that's important to my company; it's the industry standard. Leading from the front is based on the idea that each member of the team will only produce, on average, half of what their manager produces. This means that the manager in the field working the doors and the hours sets an example for their team to follow. That's a main premise for many major online knocking seminars.

But why do managers lead from the front? That is what I was trying to understand considering my stats are consistently low but those of my team are consistently high. There has to be something that everyone is missing here.

By my understanding, this we lead from the front because if we are out in the trenches with our team every day, embracing the suck, producing at high levels, we become an example to our team. That's a very important thing. We are constantly showing them the direction they should be aiming for. Also, we earn the respect of the team. No one wants to work for someone they don't respect. You don't get anyone's respect simply by being their manager. Respect is always earned, not given, and you first must earn their trust. Trust is incredibly important because it will help build and strengthen the relationship between you and your team. From what I've seen, these concepts are why the industry celebrates leading from the front and has for some time.

So, if the goal of leading from the front is for managers to be an example, set direction, earn respect, and cultivate trust, how do we attain those goals without "leading from the front"? Leading from the front is merely a path to take; it is not the destination. That means, theoretically, there are multiple paths that could achieve that same goal. The reason I would look for a new path is that leading from the front is incredibly time-consuming. So, how could I get more done within my role's capacity in the same amount of time while achieving this goal *and* producing better results? The real goal is productivity!

I'm not at all suggesting that, as leaders, we shouldn't be out in the field. We definitely should—every day if we can. We have to be proficient at the job we manage, but personally, I refer to myself as a "lead by environment" type of manager. I know this technically isn't a thing— at least, not yet. However, my understanding of an office environment is that as long as the environment represents the promises we make and is inherently meritocratic, most people will naturally work hard to get ahead if managers simply get out of their way. I know this isn't a popular opinion and is a very libertarian approach to management; however, in every office I've ever worked in, the management or the structures have been what held the team down rather than the team itself. Ask whether management practices nepotism, tenure, or favoritism. Most offices I've worked for practice all three. Again, if people are in their roles because of who they know, that means you as a manager are keeping your team from producing to their fullest potential. Most people won't try if there's nothing to aspire to.

That being said, if one of your team members isn't performing, do you simply cut them? Do you get to know them? There are some people who are lost and have no sense of direction but will outwork the entire team if they can simply work out a sense of direction or purpose. If you haven't taken the time to get to know someone, you may be missing out on something special. Remember, not everyone is on your level—yet. You have to meet them at theirs and set them on the right path.

Does your office environment help facilitate and encourage better habits and behaviors? Or is the policy that if you aren't working at a high level, you can leave? Is production more valuable than growth over time? Is there a balance? Do you, as a manager, train others to do your job or contribute to the office? Are you actively teaching the mechanics, concepts, structures, and communications necessary to lead on your level? Do you give your team passion and excitement for the future of the company? Do you hold productive people back because you don't like them or because it would be hard to lose someone in the role that they currently hold? Is that fair? What message does that send to your team? Be average and suck up to me? Is that the type of person you want to reward? What do your actions tell your team? What is the psychological effect of the hypocrisy of what you say compared to what you implement?

I maintain that if we, as leaders, are more self-aware and understanding, we can create an environment where people will naturally produce because they have purpose, direction, and meaning within a meritocratic office environment.

To further explain a culture defined by "leading from the front," I'm going to briefly review the concepts of "raising the ceiling" and "raising the floor." These are two incredibly important office concepts to understand since they each have a profound effect on the office.

Most offices are enamored with "raising the ceiling"—and for good reason. "Raising the ceiling" is taking the part of the team that has already bought in to the growth of the office and leading them to newer heights. "Raising the ceiling" is constantly getting better and more proficient as an office. It's having higher numbers every month, breaking records, and showing any other office that you mean business. This also has to do with personal production. Often the manager will go out and grind ridiculous hours to have such incredibly out-of-this-world stats that they become a legend. Once they are a legend, the prestige is then divvied up among the rest of the team, which has them working more and more consistently over time. It's definitely an incredible feat, and any leader who puts the effort into attaining that deserves every bit of recognition that comes with it.

"Raising the floor," on the other hand, is something that most offices miss. "Raising the floor" is spending a good amount of time in intense training. It's helping new people get their "sea legs." It's foregoing your personal stats to give to those who are learning and helping struggling individuals get back on track. It's having accountability structures that define where lack of production goes too far and has consequences. It's raising the minimum standard in the office and having an office environment that contributes to retention and building up personnel instead of alienating them. Not quite as flashy as "raising the ceiling," right? However, the positive impact of this method is incredible.

I touch more on this is in the "culture" chapter of this book; however, I want you to think back to the beginning of the book. My office was first in contest against Las Vegas. Then it was against Salt Lake City. Then it was against Denver. Why did those high-powered offices that were neck and neck with us drop off as we kept progressing? The answer is simple: they were playing a different game. Some offices play a month-long game, a seasonal game, or a year-long game. Ours never ends. We are playing an infinite game.

Along the same lines, why are other high-level offices dropping by the wayside? Why do some offices crush it for a couple months, hitting numbers that are insane, and some of them never recover? It's because they never cared about raising the floor.

Think about it like this. You have an awesome office in an awesome company and many people are signing up to join. You, as the manager, are spending all your time hitting high goals to increase your ceiling. You're taking the workers who have already bought in or are high-level and bringing them up a little higher. You get fantastic recognition from your company because the metrics are high. But are those metrics working toward the goal? What happened to all those new people who had so much potential when they signed up? Did you have good, intense training? Or were they left to fend for themselves? You may think that it simply takes effort to gain traction, but that's clearly not the case, and you can easily prove that if you think about when you started in the industry. Most of us weren't naturals when we started, but now that we're killing it, we have forgotten what it's like to step into an alien realm. We've forgotten about the books we read, the mentors we had, the time we put in, the money we spent. Our past becomes so disconnected from us that we begin to think that if someone's not producing, they're not even trying. That certainly wasn't the case for me.

If you remember, when I started, I worked ten-hour days, six days a week, and hardly produced anything. I even had years of a sales background before this job! I'm willing to bet most managers had a similar start instead of coming out the gates killing it. It was development over time that got us to where we are.

"Raising the ceiling" is the focus when it comes to "lead from the front" culture. That's right. It is, in fact, a culture, and that is the main issue. Leading from the front, hitting high numbers and metrics, and getting all that recognition from corporate for the effort is the epitome of work harder, not smarter. But that is what most corporations glorify. They may have the nice catch-phrases and sayings, maybe "work smarter not harder" is even one of them, but they clearly don't believe it or else they would cele-brate it. Instead, they celebrate the opposite.

Here's a dangerous issue that I've found when a corporate office solely praises leading from the front. If the spotlight is always on the management that is leading from the front, you have to realize who your audience is. These managers worked their butts off to get to where they are, and I'm willing to bet that most of them would like to move further up the ladder. When a corporate office consis-tently spotlights one management attribute, they are relaying that this is the way to get recognized. This is the way to get noticed. If you would like to play the game, you can let the rest go as long as you put up enough numbers to let upper management parade you around. When you do that, you end up with offices where all the management leads from the front. And it looks good when you see their numbers on paper; however, there is a negative side.

If all management is leading from the front, you develop "lead from the front" culture. Considering the idea behind that style is that your team will only average half of what you produce, what happens when you slow down? You built the culture that way. What happens when you burn out? I can show you what happens with various offices from my own company. They were crushing it at one point, and then most disappeared. If they didn't disappear entirely, they definitely slowed down dramatically for periods of time.

If you don't understand this concept, you don't understand that culture is the single most important thing in the office. The way that you frame and construct the culture will affect your office more than anything else. Nothing else comes even remotely close. When you frame your culture as "lead from the front," you are telling your team to follow you—and they do. They follow you into heaven, and they will just as quickly follow you into the depths of hell. You are the leader. Where are you leading them? How long can you shoulder the work of an entire office before you become bitter? How will the office view you after you've burned out? Will all that high-level work matter then? Or will they forget about you, or even replace you, because you couldn't keep up with impossible standards?

The truth is that the industry isn't looking at the correct metrics. Their value system is incredibly off if they value personal production over office production. How disconnected is the company when they're not valuing the actual metrics that work toward the goal of the company? Just like incentivizing results as opposed to incentivizing behavior, the company can just as easily incentivize burnout over the infinite game.

Now, don't get me wrong, I'm not saying that personal production isn't important. What I'm saying is that the definition of "lead from the front," in most companies, is an underdeveloped concept. In most companies, "lead from the front" is the idea that no one will work for you if you don't have personal production. That statement is not incorrect. In fact, it is incredibly correct. If you are not working as a manager or leader, your team will not work for you. That is a fact. The part of the concept that is wrong is the definition of production. Companies like to use only personal statistical production and nothing else. Therefore, if you aren't producing as much or more than the team members you lead, you are not leading from the front by their definition. The main reason companies like this definition is because they can measure it. They have stats to look at that tell them whether you are producing at a high level. They need that transparency to feel safe.

The problem is this: We lead from the front in order to lead by example, set direction, earn respect, and cultivate trust, and we get all of those things if our level of production is higher than the rest of the team. That is, in fact, correct. Again, what is not correct is the definition of "production." Production is not as short-sighted as personal statistical production. Actually, what I've come to realize, is that it is production in general that should be the definition. If you are being more productive than your team (in any area of management), you will earn every bit of what leading from the front earns you and more. You will gain a following that will want to emulate you instead of wanting to pass you up. Remember, if leading from the front is based on personal statistical production, then if someone passes you up in production, haven't they earned the right to be your boss? If someone is constantly outproducing you in that culture, don't you think they may harbor resentment and even create a following of their own?

Say instead that you framed your culture in a way that productivity is defined as all aspects of leadership. In that case, if you are productive in any capacity directed at achieving the goal, such as maintaining culture, training new employees, constructing office and individual goals, developing employees, reading and growing, research and development, scaling the office, building relationships, recruitment, *and* personal stats, don't you think people would respect you more? Don't you think that if the heaviest hitters in your office notice all the work you do on a daily basis, they would be far less likely to undercut you or try to replace you? Don't you think that if you framed the culture of your office with the correct definition of production that you would earn far more trust and respect than you would from the myopic personal stats method?

This is precisely where an office can easily shoot themselves in the foot. Think about being part of any company meeting where they don't acknowledge the offices that are having the most productivity but instead focusing solely on the managers who are "leading from the front" with personal statistical production. What does that tell the rest of your company? Is that telling the offices in better shape that they're not using the correct metrics? Is that telling any new manager in the company that they should be modeling themselves after the "lead from the front" culture that other managers live by?

It's like the definition of insanity. It has always seemed crazy to me that management doesn't look at overall stats. And I'm not talking about stats for individuals. I'm talking about stats after new things are implemented. I'm talking about stats after we follow a manager down a rabbit hole. I'm talking about stats of a management collective following the same path.

If people were actually paying attention to what happens in "lead from the front" culture, they would either turn away from it or find ways to improve it. It's all about who works harder, not smarter.

After all that, you might be surprised to hear that I'm not against the idea of leading from the front. I would like to redefine leading from the front to be in terms of productivity in the direction of the goal. That's a "lead from the front" I can get behind.

Another thing you often hear within companies is that "leaders eat last." Sounds good, right? This is yet another catchy and trendy thing that makes new management feel like they're in the right place. However, once again, I don't care what people say; I care what people do. When a manager is proving themselves in the "lead from the front" culture, they are out grinding all day every day to prove they are proficient at their job and are the right person to lead others. There are new and struggling people who are having a hard time making enough money to stay at the job long enough to get good at it. If I'm out there grinding, even if it's with these new people, and I'm knocking all the doors and taking all the appointments for my own stats, how is that morally sound? If the company already pays me a substantial amount of money, why am I taking anything extra from my own team members who need it? How does this represent "leaders eat last"? It's more like "leaders eat everything" or "leaders don't let others find food."

Also, because of this setup, the way people are trained changes. Managers are incentivized to let new and struggling people watch them as they knock on doors and get the leads. Hopefully, if new team members see someone be successful, they can pick up some good techniques, right?

The way I train is more interactive. While people learn in different ways, the more you perform a task, the more proficient you get. When I'm training, I'll knock on a couple doors just to get the ball rolling. After that, the new person will knock on every door. They will get as far into their pitch as they can go. They do as much objection handling as they can. The moment they need help, I help them overcome objections. I am there to support and get them to the finish line. They get to see how it's done as they are doing it themselves. After every door, I ask how they feel it went. Then we reflect on it. We talk about body language, the words used, how we could've handled things a little better. I break down the cues that let us know which direction to go with the pitch and why. The difference in using this type of training is astronomical.

Give me a couple days and these new setters will be on their feet. With the first method, they may never stand up. In fact, there have been times when an individual has been trained a couple of times with the first method and had little success for weeks. The day after my training, it clicks. It also helps that I'm not taking the money from them. I'm making sure they're the ones knocking on doors so they're the ones earning the appointments and money.

One of the most important objectives in working toward the goal of the company is employee retention. Considering the sales industry is a revolving door, employee retention is just as important, if not more important, than recruiting. If you can't retain new recruits, how are you possibly going to scale your office? How much time has gone by while you've only managed to keep the same number of staff members?

If you can successfully build out the floor, you will be able to retain your team. If you can retain your team, that will allow you to build a superior culture. If your culture is superior, your team will actively recruit for you. If your team is recruiting their friends and family, you have a tight-knit group that will go to war together. If this is what your office is like, when your personal statistical production drops as a leader, you will have others stepping in and picking up the slack. If the heavy hitters are burning out, others will step up or you just won't lose too much production considering you have a large and active team. This is the type of office that puts you in a position to scale. Scaling is one of the most important objectives that takes you toward the goal.

That is the downfall of "lead from the front" culture. All of the effort is put into raising the ceiling. Raising—or even maintaining—the floor is the thing that falls behind. New recruits can't get their footing and leave. The ones who start struggling have no support and eventually have to leave too. What you have left are the strong setters who are sprinting with you toward that office goal, but again, people burn out. Once you burn out, your team burns out. Once the team burns out, many times the office will nearly collapse.

Who is to blame for that? Is it the manager for not having the spine to run their office the way they know makes sense? Is it the company's fault for celebrating "lead from the front" culture and showing that to be their value system?

It seems to me that some of these methods are relics of the industry. They've worked for so long, so why reinvent the wheel? But it's a new day, and the industry has changed over time. When anything changes, everything changes. What got you here may not get you there. I tend to see a lot of practices as vestigial concepts that, at one time, built empires. That horse got us this far—but will it get you any farther? Is that horse still taking you toward the goal? Or have you grown so fond of the horse that you just can't seem to let it go?

Now, in order to juxtapose the simplicity of the industry standards, I'm going to get a little more profound and complex. I mentioned before that there is a larger list needing a method of prioritization. Mine went like this:

1. Maintain Culture
2. Train New Employees
3. Develop Existing Employees
4. Recruitment
5. Office and Individual Goals
6. Reading/Podcasts
7. Research and Development
8. Scalability
9. Team Relationship Building
10. Personal Stats

One very important thing to keep in mind is that I came into an already highly productive establishment that had minimal structure. My prioritization makes perfect sense for the establishment that I am part of. However, my prioritization—or any prioritization—should never be permanent. It should be free-flowing. If I was to build an office from the ground up, you better believe I would be leading from the front because we wouldn't have the foundation to build upon. Starting an office from the ground up requires an ungodly amount of grind and a revolving door of recruitment until you have just enough business and personnel to stick around and create a sense of foundation.

Additionally, every so often, we realize we are coasting. Coasting is never a good sign. It is incredibly common for management to build an amazing office, get it working at a high level, and then see it level out. It doesn't sound that bad, but if you have a growth mindset, this is the equivalent of being stuck. If your office is coasting, even at a high level of production, that means you have a ceiling. When you recognize a ceiling, that means you need to change. This is a very frightening concept considering no one wants to ruin a good thing. Inherently, we want to stay where we are at because of what it took to get there. One thing is for sure: when you do decide to fundamentally change the job or office, your prioritization has to change as well.

A fundamental part of managing is that you need to be proficient at the job of the team members you manage. If you aren't, no one will follow you. That's why the best restaurant managers can fill in as cooks and bartenders. If you can't mix a drink or cook a steak, your staff will laugh at you behind your back. Generally, you get a management position because you were great at the job, and now it's your job to teach it. If you have a veteran staff, the staff can help out with training and that will allow you to focus on other things. However, what happens if you fundamentally change the job of an entire team? Now that means everyone, including the veterans, have to be seen as new recruits for the office to handle the situation correctly. Your prioritization needs to reflect that. In fact, if the change is drastic enough, it may require a completely new structure.

Let me give you an example. Say your office has been coasting at a high level and you have decided to fundamentally change the way the job is done. Have you ever done the job that way before? If you haven't proficiently, then how well can you manage it? This means you have to get back in the grind in order to become proficient in the new methods. That could take some time. The office can't hold off productivity until you figure it out. Therefore, if you are grinding, you need to delegate training since it is the next most time-consuming aspect of your job. Now you have to build out structure. This means that you may have to hire a couple high-level individuals to take on training new and struggling setters for extra pay. If you are projecting that the new methods will increase sales and productivity, that should theoretically be fine.

If you can successfully teach and hand off your ability to train, that can move farther down your prioritization list. It will mean everything to your team members to see you grind during fundamental changes. It shows that you, as a leader, believe in the changes and are invested in continuing to lead by example. During this time, your prioritization may look more like this:

1. Maintain Culture
2. Personal Stats
3. Recruitment
4. Office and Individual Goals
5. Team Relationship Building
6. Train New Employees

7. Develop Existing Employees
8. Reading/Podcasts
9. Research and Development
10. Scalability

There is nothing more important to me than maintaining culture. Culture is the number-one contributing factor to office productivity in my mind, and I would be hard-pressed to change that from being number one on the list at any given time.

But overall, the list looks quite a bit different than before. So, what does all of this mean? This means that an entire industry can't be as simple as a one-trick pony. I don't only mean that for "lead from the front" management; I also mean having a permanent prioritization. If you want to be a leader on another level who runs an office that constantly raises the ceiling for what it can potentially produce, you need to be versatile! You have to be able to diagnose what is needed within your office at any given time and restructure your prioritization accordingly. An office is a living, breathing thing that grows and changes. Depending on the phase your office is in, you will always have to be the right person to lead it. That means that your productivity (as defined by all the different aspects of leadership) has to remain high, and your prioritization has to be in the correct order for the current office phase.

Do you want your office to get to the next step? Then redefine the metrics. Leading from the front should no longer be bound solely to personal statistical production. Leading from the front should mean any production that takes you closer to the goal.

Again, the goal of the company is to make money. The goal of the office is to be productive. If you run an office, your job is to make the office productive. If you haven't constructed a value system with prioritization, you're working in the abstract. Take all the jobs and tasks and structures you have and run them through the process of negative. Do those things work to bring you toward the goal? If not, get rid of them or change them. Prioritize what you have left and structure them into a value system. Be versatile. Be aware that change is inevitable and we never have all the answers. Continue doing the things that bring you closest to the goal in all phases. Balance these things. Of course, they will all be important, but it will become very clear where you should be spending most of your productivity when you have these ideas built out.

Remember, no structures, concepts, or methods will ever be perfect. Don't be afraid to challenge, expand, or even change things. If no one ever dared to speak up, there would never be innovation. If you happen to understand something differently than those who came before you, there is immense value in that. You may be on the verge of changing the game entirely. It would be sad to think that someone deserving never changed the game because they were afraid to challenge the status quo. Don't give in to the door-to-door dogma just because that's the way things have always been done.

Chapter 8:

Managerial Styles

This is a chapter that goes hand in hand with both Creative Control and Door-to-Door Dogma. Generally, when a manager moves up, they tend to replace themselves with a clone. Of course this is completely natural. If you handled the job to the best of your abilities, it only makes sense to leave someone in the role who does everything exactly the same way you did.

Of course, that doesn't necessarily mean that another type of manager can't do the job well differently. In fact, there are many different types of managers who can expand the job in different directions and improve on areas that were lacking.

In this chapter, I'm going to break down what I consider to be the six main managerial styles, how they each contribute, and the synergy between them. Perhaps you will find your style on this list. Personally, I believe everyone has a mixture of styles. Very rarely will you find someone proficient in all styles, although that is technically the goal. Let your strength take you into the stratosphere and then learn and grow as much as you can. The more styles you collect, the more valuable you become.

I also expand on "raising the ceiling" and "raising the floor" in this chapter. I go over how the different styles contribute to the support of and competitiveness in the office.

Raising the ceiling, of course, is bringing the office to new heights. It's focusing on motivating the heavy hitters to grind. It's focusing on efficiencies like close rate and rate of appointments held. Raising the ceiling is showing the rest of the world what a champion looks like. It's raising the bar so high that it seems out of reach for anyone who would even dare attempt it. Raising the ceiling is flashy and comes with a lot of prestige. It makes you a legend in your company as well as your industry. Due to all that, it is the single most sought-after habit a company will look for in office management. Raising the ceiling is generally achieved through competition, whether that's competition within the offices such as heavy hitters pitted against each other, competition against another office, or competition against another company in the industry, competition is what motivates the driven to go to war.

Raising the floor, on the other hand, is the support required to intensely train the new and struggling workers. It's focusing on getting new members their "sea legs" and finding the missing puzzle pieces that can turn struggling individuals into average or even powerhouse workers. Raising the floor is allowing people who are not used to the industry to make just enough money that they can continue long enough to gain some traction. This builds a strong foundation for your office so that it doesn't drop off if the top producers burn out. This will allow you to have a larger team and outproduce any other office without having any heavy hitters. And imagine what it would be like with heavy hitters.

There is zero flash in raising the floor. In fact, most companies would stick their nose in and ask why you are wasting your time on people who "aren't going to make it." Nearly everyone can make it; we just need to figure out how. Raising the floor is achieved through support and training. Whether that is done through intensive training, one-on-one training, helping individuals get past personal problems, or just helping them find their motivation in life, support is required to keep an office self-sustaining. It also breeds loyalty.

What's more important: production now or growth over time? If you're an infinite gamer, you may say growth over time. The truth is that you have to find a balance. You can't overlook being productive now, but growth over time will allow you to continuously produce more. Those are both incredibly important to the goal!

So, how do managers differ in their approaches within this field? How do they contribute in their own way? I'll start with the most common management style. Here I am not using common as a negative term, rather, it's most common because it's imperative to keeping things up and running.

The Administrator:

The Administrator is the glue that keeps the office together. The administrator is who enforces the structures within the office. If there's someone falling behind in their metrics, the administrator will point it out. It's the same deal if someone is exceeding the metrics and needs to move up. The administrator was the teacher's pet who was picked on in high school because they did everything by the book. Then they grow up to be administrators. They build the slideshows. They put out the incentives on time. They order the prizes for the incentives. They make sure the meetings don't go over the time limit. The Administrator watches the statistics and advises others about who needs help and what methods were used before in the same situation. If there's an issue with payroll, if there's an issue from another department, if there's any communication that needs to be had, this is the person who will pick that up.

When it comes to raising the ceiling and raising the floor, the administrator is neutral. There are procedures for both, and they simply follow the procedures. There is no need to reinvent the wheel.

Without this style of manager, the office would be lost. Managers who are shooting for the moon or who are trying to reinforce the fort need to be reminded of how much money is in the office budget. They need to be reminded which procedures didn't work the first time so they don't get repeated. The downside to being an administrator is that they tend to be referred to as the "ivory tower" managers. There will always be an administrator in every office because it's absolutely necessary. Even if someone isn't naturally one, they will learn to take this role.

The Motivator:

The Motivator is a powerful force in an office. The Motivator is fiery and has so much heart. They are there to build up the team in public and the individual in private. Throw all those motivational videos out the window. Those videos only get people psyched up for an hour. If you can bring that fire to the team yourself, it will turn into a blaze!

The definition of sales is the transference of belief. The Motivator gives that to their team. That feeling and drive lasts so much longer if it's brought genuinely by an individual. Because of this, the Motivator is an incredibly valuable asset many offices try to replicate with online videos. This is the type of manager who has a major impact on the office culture and has the team wanting to come to meetings. That's a hard thing to find.

The Motivator primarily raises the ceiling. Firing up the team will get the average producers knocking on doors longer and the heavy hitters producing an extra 10 percent. They are the war generals who are leading the charge and bringing the office to new heights authentically.

The Motivator is a naturally passionate person. The danger of this type of manager is that passion is a neutral tool. If they corrupt their passion with ego, condescension, or anger, the floor will fall out. The passion of a negative Motivator can keep the team from expanding, holding on to only the core producers. If the Motivator replaces those negative attributes with heart, they will build up everyone around them. In fact, a positive Motivator can touch even struggling workers that other management has given up on. Though, generally, that's normally a rare thing. For the most part, the Motivator doesn't spend too much time on the support side. Motivators generally lead from the front and are invaluable to a company.

The Rabbit:

I know, it sounds like we're getting into zodiac signs, but the rabbit is definitely a sought-after manager. Why does anyone get promoted? Generally, they get promoted because they were proficient at the job. If someone is more proficient at the job than everyone else, that person has a very strong shot at being a manager. If that manager continues to show up everyone on the team while also managing, that person is a Rabbit.

The Rabbit is the embodiment of "lead from the front" mentality. The Rabbit is productive on a personal level that far exceeds the production of literally anyone else. If someone on the team is generating fifteen appointments a week, the Rabbit will do thirty. Then they'll do it the next week and the week after that. If a CEO is reading this, I'm sure you're salivating right about now. Upper management likes to be able to keep tabs through statistics. The Rabbit is a favorite because you can always look to the stats and know they're producing at a high level. There's no guessing whether they're working or not.

A negative thing about a Rabbit is in part due to the upper management. A Rabbit can easily be used as a smoke screen if the office isn't producing quite on the level that it should. Management can just point to the stats and say, "Hey, that manager never sleeps" instead of trying to find an underlying cause for low production. That's not the Rabbit's fault, but it does hurt the Rabbit.

Another negative thing about the Rabbit is that because they are collecting personal statistics, they tend not to train new and struggling people to the level they need to reach in order to get by. They may be strengthening the ceiling, but they tend to neglect the floor.

Generally, the Rabbit will be running with the heavy hitters, leading the charge. The Rabbit brings up the average and heavy hitters because they are in the trenches with them. No one questions their leadership because they can't touch their stats. However, if your worth as a manager is tied exclusively to stats, then when someone comes along who can outproduce you, they will challenge you.

The Support:

The Support role is probably the most overlooked role. The Support does nothing flashy and there's very little to measure their contribution. It's definitely not a management style that turns heads or make your team go to war. Basically, the Support manager is there to exclusively build the floor. This manager teaches the basics and trains the newbies. This is the manager who takes people out and helps them do their own work. Then they will reflect on that work. How do we make this better? How can we say what you said better? Do you notice their body language and the things they said? The Support helps show people a quicker way of getting into an industry that some haven't experienced before. They also tend to hand any appointments off to the team so that they can make enough money to keep going.

While the Support role doesn't get much recognition, you can determine their contribution through the consistency of the office. If you're entirely focused on building the floor, by nature, you will retain many of the new hires and grow a bigger team. Even if the members of this team aren't super productive on an individual level, you will have enough bodies to sustain production.

The downside to this leadership style is that the team has no example of a heavy hitter to follow. If you're completely tied up in training, you rarely have enough time to go out and gain stats. Your office will likely have a ton of average individuals with hardly any heavy hitters.

Don't sleep on this method. Most offices burn out because they can't keep consistently high productivity. The Support manager's team will not burn out.

The Innovator:

This is what I consider myself. Technically, I also fill the Administrator and Support role in my office, but that's due to necessity. I am definitely an Innovator at heart.

The Innovator likes change. The Innovator wants to see which actions and words create results. However, instead of using those stats to teach lessons, the Innovator uses those stats to build structures within the office. This management style wants to expand upon existing structures, create new structures, introduce new methods, and have all of these things be arranged in a way that creates synergy. Sometimes things don't play out, but the Innovator sees that as something they now know that they didn't before. They take what they can learn from it and go another direction.

The Innovator is easily the least sought-after style of management in most places. This is partly due to the fact that any changes can feel like a challenge to the ego of other managers. Of course, all managers have their own structure that they work by, so when someone comes in and starts shaking things up, it's hard not to see them as going overboard or "reinventing the wheel." This causes a lot of frustration and makes it incredibly hard for other managers to accept them.

There is definitely need for skepticism when it comes to an Innovator. The world of sales and business has been around forever. If someone who is naturally an Innovator but lacks experience comes in and tries to change everything, there's a good chance they will try things that have failed in the past. If the Innovator is merely creating with ideas and no data, they can really ruin an office fast. This can make this manager fairly volatile. For this style to work correctly, you have to constantly be in research and development mode. You need to be paying close attention to stats and the nature of your workers, as well as your co-managers. In fact, you may only be able to implement things that work in your specific group.

The Innovator is neutral when it comes to raising the ceiling or floor. They will imagine structures and procedures for both. The hard part is selling those structures and procedures to your team. Good luck!

The Stoic:

The Stoic is neutral and thinks neutrally. The Stoic has a plan for the future but lives in the moment. This manager tends to follow statistics but uses them primarily for lessons and team building. The policies are what they are, and there should never be an exception. Everyone needs to know that no one gets special treatment. The Stoic is quick to listen and slow to speak, which adds gravity to their words. This makes this type of manager a natural leader, not only for the team but for the other managers as well.

The Stoic is not against change, though they are skeptical of it. There has to be very solid data for change, and it has to be bought about by the team. This makes new policies and procedures move fairly slowly unless the Stoic can be sold on them. This is a "jack of all trades, master of none" style of managing. They tend to be well-versed across the board in all the different aspects of managing. They generally are not well-versed enough to be the best but are strong enough to teach. It may be that in the event someone quits or gets fired, the Stoic can fill any position. This makes them a rock. If there is anything lacking in any general area, it will be covered until someone else can take over. This type of manager is fantastic for handling issues as they arise. New problems mean we are moving in the right direction. That's a valuable manager to have.

***

This may seem like a strange chapter so far considering I'm breaking down and categorizing management styles from my perspective, yet it's important to understand the diversity of prioritization different people have. Again, many times when a manager gets promoted, they will try to fill their previous position with someone who holds an identical prioritization. That doesn't mean that the other management styles aren't able to do the job correctly. They simply prioritize other aspects. In fact, if there are only two or three managers, those managers will fill all the gaps and take on multiple roles to cover all their bases. Generally, people don't become a certain style just because that's what they are the best at. People take on a style and become proficient at it because they feel that is the most important role. It's at the top of their value system.

Generally, if you only have two or three managers, you don't want to be teamed up with someone who has an identical style or focus. For example, if you are a Motivator, you may not want to team up with a Rabbit. You will both focus on the top producers and create some all-stars, but you will tend not to grow as a team. The floor won't be built out.

Similarly, if you're an Administrator, you may not want to team up with a Support manager. Then the top producers aren't being motivated or reaching to their fullest potential. You would build out a large team of average or below average workers. The major downside is that without an example of what success looks like in the office, there's not going to be much perception of opportunity, so your team members may not even try to become heavy hitters. You need to either be an example or have examples in the office. This will naturally give the team something to aspire toward.

Again, naturally I am an Innovator. The person I replaced did all of the administrative work for the office, so when I came in, I took on the administration side. I was paired with a Motivator, which is fantastic considering that's a skill I didn't possess. Since this Motivator likes to lead from the front and work with the top producers, I decided to spend most of my free time working on building out the floor. I did this, of course, because I understand the balance necessary to expand the office.

If you have a strong team of heavy hitters, along with a good foundation of people to work with, you can focus on the culture of your office. Once the culture of your office is good, the team will actively recruit their friends and family. The more friends and family, the stronger the connection of the team. Once you have this steady flow of recruitment, it will allow you to then scale your office.

Basically, if the goal of the office is productivity and you can get the office productive and self-sustaining, you can then scale the office, which will rapidly increase the productivity of your office. Doing this can be difficult if you are pigeonholing yourself in one management style. Therefore, your management goal is to become proficient in all management styles so that you can be the right person to lead your office into the next phase of the company. If you become that manager, you're going to have a bright future.

Chapter 9:

Statistical Roadmaps

Every office is different. Every once in a while, someone will ask me for all the structures I use so they can quickly implement them in their offices. Unfortunately, that can end up being a train wreck, especially considering how new the office is. If your office is just starting out, you will have to build those out over time as you need them. Also, considering your culture and your team, my structures may be a little different than the structures your office needs. The funny thing is that everyone has data that shows them what their office needs—in the form of statistics.

If your office doesn't keep statistics, you are greatly hindering your office's improvement as well as your own. The mistake I see most people make is that they merely look at statistics as an abacus to tally the score. When the stats are high, we are excited! When the stats are low, we are frustrated and ask what we can do to get the stats back on track. I have seen so many conversations about why the stats might be low where no one really has an idea why.

The statistics will show you!

The statistics are a roadmap to orient us toward the goal. They can tell you what motivates your team, how to motivate the team, and when to motivate the team. Statistics will also show you the opposite. They will show you what doesn't motivate your team, the procedures that hurt the motivation of your team, and when *not* to motivate you team.

Well, that seems weird, right? When would you not want to motivate your team? Let me bring up an earlier example.

When running incentives, I've talked about what I call "reactive incentives." A reactive incentive is something like when the day isn't quite going the way you'd like it to, you throw out an incentive toward the second half of the day to milk whatever last productivity you can get from the team. Every time I have ran a reactive incentive, there is no data that shows an increase in the team's productivity. This is most likely because the team has already chosen what their day is going to be like. Now you're paying extra money for no extra work. The real negative byproduct of this type of incentive is that if the team or individual does not hit the intended goal, the team will work even less the next day because they either get disheartened or see management as desperate.

It may seem crazy for me to say that it can affect the next day like that; however, every single time I have ran a reactive incentive, that is the result. Even though I don't like using reactive incentives at all, from time to time, I run one just to see that result play out. It's always good to replicate what you know so that everyone can understand how the statistics work.

With the information learned from statistics, I know never to run reactive incentives. Now I have a learned behavior that benefits the office. That's a tool I now have forever. The more statistical tools you have in your toolbox, the smoother your office will run, and the more sustainable it will be.

Again, if you don't have statistics or have very few statistics, I urge you to start keeping stats for as many things as you can. How many leads do individuals set? Daily? Weekly? Monthly? How many of those appointments are held? How many of those appointments end up buying? Of all the appointments that didn't get held, what was the reason?

Do you think that all of that information is pointless? Why would someone keep track of all of those things?

Let me show you what I can learn from all of this.

Keep in mind, I work in the solar industry, so some of what I'm going to go over may not seem applicable, but the methods are the important part.

In my office, I have a breakdown that tallies what happens with each lead. How many of the leads were held goes toward a positive percentage. With the remainder that weren't held, did the lead reschedule, cancel with the setter, or cancel at the door? Maybe the setter is saying too much at the door or not setting a good enough expectation.

Was the lead canceled because the home didn't get enough sun to benefit from solar? Was the customer a renter? Were they leaving within a year? Was the appointment with only one decision-maker? Then the setter needs to qualify better when they're setting up appointments. Did the homeowner forget or were they simply not home? The setter may have forgotten to follow up.

I have all of these outcomes tallied in a line item I call "blind spot." This represents the main issue each individual has. That allows me to better manage on an individual level and really give my team the attention and training they deserve—and need—to be successful. If they don't show a blind spot, I check how many appointments have been set by that person. I'm willing to bet their blind spot is working the hours. The more productive you are, the more problems you're going to have. In fact, I tend not to get too upset if a setter runs into problems; we can always rein it in. I'm more worried if they never have problems.

If a setter's stats are through-the-roof positive, like they have an incredibly high rate of appointments held, have that person speak to your team. Even as leaders, we don't have all the answers. We also don't need to be the focus of all motivation. If you praise members of the team for good work, others will work for recognition as well. It's incredibly important to recognize when someone on the team is having a moment of brilliance. They might not even know why they're doing well, but if you have them explain their process to the group, you or another member of the team may be able to pinpoint the reason for their success and replicate it.

What about on the closer side? How many appointments do they have on their calendar each week? How many of those appointments did that closer sit with? Does that matter? Well, if the closer is sitting with as many customers as possible, yet their close rate is low, doesn't that closer need coaching? There may be something wrong with their presentation or current skills as a salesperson. Maybe they're sitting appointments that shouldn't be held, for example, if only one of multiple decision-makers are present. On the other hand, if that person isn't sitting with many of their appointments, is that only recently or is that a pattern over time? If it's a recent development, perhaps it's an issue with the leads that are being set. If it's a pattern over time, there's a good chance that the closer is cherry-picking the leads and only going after the low-hanging fruit. How would we know to look at that if there was no statistical data?

What structures or ideas are motivating your closer team? Do you see your team selling more or less when you compare your team to another office? How are you comparing them? Are you comparing them out of jealousy or are you comparing yourselves competitively? Watch the stats. Do it again, and watch the stats again. Is this a pattern of behavior or a one-time thing? What information can you take from this?

A great example of from my office is when we have a day that the ratios are really off. It's incredibly important to understand how interconnected all departments are. What one department does or doesn't do will affect the others. In fact, sometimes departments will try to disconnect from the other departments out of frustration. When this happens, you will notice one department taking off but others start to decline because there is no communication or structures in place to make these departments work together on a productive level.

The following example from my office may seem subtle, but it had a strong effect on the office. In my office, the setter teams hover around a 45 percent rate of appointments held. The close rate on setter leads stays around 35 percent, while the overall close rate is about 45 percent. Normally, our departments run like a well-oiled machine. The setters are setting appointments, and the closers are closing. We are very productive. Every once in a while, there will be a day or so when the ratios aren't as great. Recently, we had a day where we had twenty-three held appointments and only four of them closed. This is fairly rare for our office. If we have twenty-three held appointments, we should at the very least have ten of them closed. One of the closer managers addressed the team and said that this was unacceptable. This is an understandable position to take if you hold your team in high regard. He went on to say that if we couldn't close given that much opportunity, those closers would have the privilege of leads taken away from them.

Think about this for a moment. Is this manager wrong to work this way? Technically, the team had a terrible day of production that most managers would—and should—see as unacceptable. Is taking leads away the right method if individuals can't keep their sales up? There's definitely an argument for that. However, how do we implement that correctly? How do we present that in a way that doesn't harm morale? You may think that the method used wouldn't harm, but here's what happened.

If you address your team and tell them there will be repercussions based on ratios, what exactly are you incentivizing your team to do? You're incentivizing them to fix the ratios. That hopefully means they will try harder to close their appointments; however, if they don't, they will likely mark their appointments as not being held or begin stringently cherry-picking through the appointments they are given. That means that if they show up to an appointment and feel it out and decide that they have a low chance of closing it, they will just walk away. Now they're only focused on closing the low-hanging fruit so they won't lose the privilege of having leads.

If you were to pay attention to the stats during this time, you would see what I call "flipping the ratios." When the closers cherry-pick their appointments, you will see their close rate go up and the appointments held rate go way down. They've flipped. In fact, the appointments held rate in our office went from 45 percent to 35 percent while the closer rate on setter leads went from 35 percent to 45 percent.

If you were managing the closer team during this time, you may be excited that your closers are closing at such a high rate! This, however, is not clear metric that benefits you. Is that high close rate getting you closer to the goal? What was the goal again? Oh yeah, productivity.

When the ratios flipped and the close percentage went up 10 percent, the appointments held percentage was down by 10 percent. Due to this, the office productivity went down approximately 20 percent. Not only that, but the setter team gets paid by appointments held. That means that they were getting paid less and being disincentivized to work as hard as they were. There was no reason to work as hard as they were if the other department wasn't taking care of them. All of this was shown in the statistics and let us know how to react to our team moving forward. There must be a better way to keep productivity sustainable. That method, however, was not it.

When you treat individuals a certain way, how does that affect their performance? Do you downplay their successes as not being enough? That motivates some people but will ruin the motivation of others. Are you complementing them on their talent or work ethic? The way you compliment people greatly changes their future success.

How do your teams react to each other? How does that affect your office? You might ask how to measure that, and that's why you have to pay attention. Whenever you notice a shift in the office, whether that's culture or interactions, watch the stats. Record what is happening. You may not have any conclusions the first time it happens, but you record it so you can compare the results the next time it happens. That's how we learn and understand things on a much more detailed level.

Why does your office run incentives? The clear answer is to incentivize people to work more. Of course, as I mentioned in Chapter 3, I use incentives to gain information as well. I've used what I've learned from previous statistics to create new incentives. Then, from those incentives, I gain more information for future use.

Does your office work better with team incentives or individual incentives? What types of prizes work better? How much production is too little or too much to ask for? When do we enact these incentives? What time of day? Which day of the week? Which week of the month? How long do we run the incentives? How much information can we gain about our team through the incentive?

Personally, I like to use as few incentives as possible. That makes it far easier to gain information about what you're running. You have to be able to attribute your stats to one thing, and if you're running too many things at one time, it's hard to say what is really affecting your team. You want to make your stats as simple and clear as possible.

One thing I've noticed about my office is that normally our Mondays are highly productive, but our Tuesdays are not. However, every once in a while, our Monday will be good and our Tuesday will be incredible. Every time that has happened, my team has held that high production through Thursday and then that production falls off on Friday and most likely Saturday. Now, every time I see that productive Tuesday, I do not run any incentives throughout the week because the team will work anyway, then I will post an incentive on Friday night for Saturday. Again, through the knowledge I gained from statistics, I have made these particular incentives for teams of two and generally for apparel such as shoes or sunglasses. This is all learned from statistics that I've collected over time. By doing this, we have consistently maintained high production on Saturdays during these particular weeks.

In learning, understanding, and using statistics, you can really begin to see which processes and structures move you toward the goal. If you hold individuals or your team accountable, do they become more productive? Does a change in your office culture affect productivity? When you implement structures that offer status, how does that affect productivity? When you implement opportunities that require clear metrics, how does that affect productivity? The statistics are a clear roadmap that can easily show you which structures you should create and how to implement them.

One structure that I have been campaigning for in my office is having an accountability structure for our closer team. At the time of writing this book, if you become a closer, you stay a closer no matter how low your production is. There is no minimum standard and no system of accountability to keep them from falling below a specific metric.

Back in December of 2020, we created a meritocracy structure for the department. We did this by taking the stats from the previous week and restructuring who gets the most leads the next week based on production. The stats from the two weeks prior to implementing this structure were a 48 percent rate on appointments held with a 33 percent close rate. The two weeks after we implemented this structure were 55 percent on appointments held and 43 percent closed. This means that when the closer team feels accountability, the close rate *and* the appointments held went up significantly!

The unfortunate thing was that by the time January hit, our setter team was producing so many leads that there was no longer a meritocracy system. Every closer had their days filled from there on out, and their close percentage on setter leads dropped back down. This, of course, teaches us that a balance of leads to closers that allows for meritocracy will incentivize more production.

The concept of productivity by accountability was validated again in January. At the beginning of January, we notified the closer department that if they dropped below a certain metric for the month, they would no longer receive appointments from the company and would have to prospect appointments on their own. Through the first three weeks of the month, the rate of appointments held was 42 percent while the close rate on setter appointments was only 28 percent. That is an incredibly low rate to have for three weeks. The very last week of the month, there were many closers who would have lost their job, so we saw the production ramp up from fear of losing that privilege. The rate of appointments held went up to 43 percent and the close rate went up to 48 percent! That's 20 percent higher than the previous three weeks! Knowing those metrics, I knew we absolutely had to implement a regular structure of accountability.

At the end of that month, no one had lost their privileges—not because everyone hit the metrics, but because as a management team, we were afraid to lose opportunity. We had so many leads coming in that we couldn't run them all. The issue with this fear is that opportunity doesn't always translate to productivity. While it's true that we would lose opportunity for one month, if the rest of the team recognized how important maintaining their productivity was, the team as a whole would be more productive with less opportunity. Then we could focus on more opportunity.

Expanding on this idea, I wanted to try something. For one Saturday, I changed the appointment schedule so that the appointments for each closer were at least three hours apart. Basically, if a closer had their first appointment at 10 a.m., their next one would be at 1 p.m. and then 4 p.m. I made sure that each individual had a three-hour window from one to the next. I wanted to make sure that the closer could account for drive time to the appointment and time to write up the sale if they had made it. I thought that if we didn't give closers enough time between appointments, they might not really be giving their best at each one or they might be incentivized to rush through them so that they could simply get to the next appointment.

That particular Saturday, we had a low number of appointments. We normally have about fifty appointments. That Saturday, we only had thirty-seven. By the end of the day, we had twenty-four of the appointments held and seventeen of them had closed. It was one of the most productive days in company history for an office. We had corporate calling to cheer us on to hopefully break previous records.

I began comparing this Saturday to days we had previously in the week and then against the Saturdays we worked in previous months, and I found some very interesting information. The days in which we had fifty-plus appointments, where appointments were crowded within two hours of each other, we had very few appointments held as well as appointments sold. On the days we had fewer appointments but structured the days with enough time for our team to work them better, we had a much higher percentage of appointments held as well as appointments sold.

So, what does this mean?

I decided to take this back a lot further. In August 2020, our office had the best month in sales that it's had to date. We had 214 sales from 340 appointments held. Now, the very next month, all stats declined; however, if you look at every month after September, we have had more appointments held with less sales.

Well, that was very strange, and I wanted to know what it meant.

When I compared what happened since August 2020 to what I learned in my scheduling experiment, I came to realize something.

> An increase in opportunity does not equate to an increase in productivity.

This seemed like a counterintuitive concept to me. I was under the impression that my job as a manager was strictly to bring in opportunity for the office to take advantage of. Our office sure has an abundance of opportunity, but that hasn't been moving the needle toward the goal. We can't just throw everything at the wall and see what sticks. We shouldn't solely be looking at how much we are working but how we are working. This goes back to work smarter, not harder. Perhaps on the setter side, we bring in less appointments but set up those appointments better. On the closer side, we need take our time and not cut corners. This means that execution takes precedence.

Maybe we then look at the entire office that way. We have built up a large team and are self-sustaining to the point that we can scale. If we scale now, however, does that mean that we are only scaling the opportunity?

Well, if we've found that opportunity hasn't contributed to production, maybe that's not the correct way to go. Maybe before we begin to scale, we need to focus on the execution of the office first. When we have a certain threshold of statistics met consistently, then we should scale.

Nearly everything I've written about in this book has been learned through statistics. I highly urge everyone to really pay attention to anything that affects your team statistically. When you attempt any of the systems and procedures in this book, validate them with statistics. You may even find better ways to alter them. Take a look at what is and isn't working in your office and use the statistical roadmaps to your advantage in building out better structures to take your office to new heights!

Chapter 10

Managing versus Leading

A fter what we learned from the statistics, we know we need to change the way our team works on a funda- mental level. That is not an easy task by any means. In fact, fundamentally changing a job is an easy way to lose a good portion of your team. But considering we now know that execu- tion is far more important than opportunity, we need to focus on cutting down on poor opportunities, learning how to make more opportunities winning opportunities, and then scaling from there. This, of course, is going to create fear because the first thing we associate with this plan is less opportunity to make money. Uncertainty comes with a fundamental change at any job, and uncertainty then becomes lack of motivation. As management, we have to be conscious and understanding of that. However, the setter team doesn't get paid for leads generated, they get paid for appointments held. Therefore, we theoretically could generate less leads and create more and better business while simultaneously not wasting the closers' time.

Now, of course, the increase in execution applies to the closer side as well. In fact, execution needs to be the focus on all ends. The management, the scheduling, the closers, and the setters all need to focus on new policies that will move them toward better execution. If we move toward better execution, that moves us in the direction of the goal.

While on the closer side we are implementing more training and accountability, on the setter side, we are changing the way they do their day-to-day work.

The way we have had the setter team work ever since I've been here is everyone has full control of their job. If they work, they work; if they don't, they don't. We don't tell them where to work either. They pick a neighborhood the day before and spend however much time they want in that neighborhood. Generally, they move to a different neighborhood every day. It's free reign.

Since I've been here, that's seemed like a no-brainer. Our setter team is the most consistent in the company, so there's clearly been no reason to change the way they work. If the deals aren't closing, that's not on my department, that's on the closer department. My job is to get them in the doors.

If we look at the heaviest hitters in the industry, they tend to put one person in an area for an elongated period of time, about one to three months. Looking through the lens of better execution, what could be the benefits of working that way? Well, people tend to say "yes" to appointments if they feel comfortable with you. So, if we have the same person in one area, people will begin to recognize that person. That could definitely be a benefit. If that setter is able to set up an appointment that sells, they can use that customer's name as they knock on other doors in the area. In fact, as a job is installed, they can knock on doors around that area and if enough get installed in a certain amount of time, neighbors are going to consistently see the same person over and over again while seeing their neighbors take advantage of the program. In a way, it's like leaving no stone unturned.

We were allowing everyone to choose their areas because there is quite a lot of low-hanging fruit and our numbers have always been fantastic. However, this method should get all the low-hanging fruit while also turning other homeowners into reachable fruit.

If we switch to a style like this, we have to learn how to teach it well. We also will have to rebrand the position as being something far more professional. You are not simply knocking on doors here; you are building a brand. You are the CEO of your own company. You need business cards. You need to take ownership of your job. You need to have intent behind every action.

In fact, if you become this person and this is your neighborhood, then when appointments don't get held, you can swing back by the house and get them set up again considering you are always in their neighborhood. This is a style meant to milk a neighborhood for everything that it has.

So, let's roll this out to the team. How your team reacts to a fundamental change in their work will show you whether you are a manager or a leader.

Have you ever worked at a company, even one not in sales, and that company drastically changed the way things have always been done? Most of the time, people sigh and complain. You think there's no reason they have to switch everything up. The company is doing just fine. I've had that happen a couple times in my life, and I've almost always been upset about it. Of course, I've never had leaders in my life.

A manager is someone who handles the day-to-day. They make sure the numbers are at least decent. They praise and they discipline. When things change, they say, "This is what's happening. Deal with it." The manager makes sure that everyone adheres to the new policies and protocols. Whatever happens, happens. A manager tells their workers what to do and they do it. A normal go-to for a manager rolling out a fundamental change is to pin it on corporate, saying something like, "Corporate is changing everything. I did what I could but we're going to start transition to this new method." This takes the pressure off the manager if it's not a popular change. You're just one of the guys when this happens.

A leader, on the other hand, is someone people follow. A leader will show you the light, saying things like, "This policy change is a natural progression and evolution of the position and it's going to make you so much more money than you thought you could make here. It's going to be more fulfilling, practical, manageable, and efficient." The leader believes in the change, so they can sell the change to their team. If you can get your team to believe in it, or better yet, if the team has already bought into you as a leader and will follow you no matter what, you will retain your team and have them excited to go into the new phase. A leader will take ownership of the new phase, "We have done incredibly well so far but the direction I'm taking you is going to make us tower among the competition! After we execute this correctly, there won't even be competition!" The team will be excited to make that journey with you.

When I put together the statistics at the end of Chapter 9 and they showed that execution should be the primary focus, I took those statistics to my team. I walked them through the stats and asked them if they noticed any trends. Of course, my team isn't a group of managers, they are a group of setters, but we have an incredible group of minds. I showed various stats until people started piping up. They began to say that it looked like they could be doing better. At first, they weren't sure if it was a setter or closer problem but very soon started saying that they could strive to be more professional.

I hit them with my realization that an increase in opportunity doesn't equate to an increase in productivity. They then started coming up with new ideas, talking amongst themselves. You could see them over the course of an hour moving toward the thought of farming neighborhoods instead of blitzing them as we have been. They began pondering how to be more professional and all the different ways they could start evolving the way they work. They were selling themselves on the idea that we were going to roll out to them anyway!

Being a leader is not an easy thing to learn. If you have made a journey and come to a realization, many people will not understand your conclusion if they don't make the same journey. This is true for any of us; I'm no exception.

A good example is when I started managing here. I was working on an issue that seemed to have no positivity to it at all. I wanted to be rid of it so that it was no longer a focus, but there were others who didn't want to be rid of it. They saw value in it that I hadn't. I tried breaking this issue down various times with my boss, Asia. I didn't believe that her choice to keep this particular aspect of the office had any merit, and it didn't make sense. She told me, "You need to stop seeing everything in black and white and start seeing things in shades of gray." Then I was frustrated and had a riddle to solve. Actually, my first interpretation of this line was that she didn't want me to question her when she made mistakes.

Clearly, I'm very confident in my own understanding.

As time went on, there were issues stemming from the same kind of misunderstanding. I couldn't understand why we would be so patient with things that seemed so toxic. I would constantly argue with my boss about things, and she would calmly say the same thing, "You need to stop seeing things in black and white and start seeing things in shades of gray."

One night we were having dinner while going over office issues. She dropped that line one more time and I said something back, "Asia, every time you say that to me, I trust you less." She definitely got wide-eyed and wasn't sure how to respond. I responded this way because the only understanding I could come up with was, again, that she was just diverting my focus when she made mistakes.

One night, I was in the middle of reading a book called *The Vision Driven Leader* by Michael Hyatt. In this book, Michael Hyatt dropped Asia's line in a slightly different way. Paraphrased, he said that managers lack the ability to see the world in shades of gray. I immediately realized I needed to figure this out. So I looked online and read a few different stories and understandings of the line. Basically, it's just saying that no matter how bad things seem, there is a silver lining we can always improve upon. I realized what I had been seeing as stupidity was really patience. I've never known companies to be patient with anything or anyone that wasn't producing positive results. In fact, normally those things are gone fairly quickly. But here I was working for a company that cares so much about personal growth that they are overly patient with people to get there. This also means they had to be patient with me as I solve their riddles.

Without the leadership of Asia in particular, I wouldn't be nearly the leader I am today. Now it's my job to be a leader to others.

So how does one lead others? Honestly, we're all a work in progress. To lead, we need to be further along in our process than others. A teacher has read more books and learned more things than you have. That's why they are teaching you. It's very similar with the leadership process. How quickly can you learn and grow and change perspectives? If you follow the process of self-improvement, you will quickly realize that it doesn't end. We are never anywhere near our full potential to lead. That idea will give anyone a sense of humility.

In fact, there have been a few times when I've been hit hard with these realizations. I generally put in a lot of work. I'm a highly productive person in a lot of ways, and sometimes I get close to a place where I begin to feel like I have everything figured out and I'm on top of the world. When you approach a peak like this, get ready, because you will have moments that shatter your whole perspective and bring you all the way back down to the beginning.

I had that happen once when I was twenty-seven years old, before I ever went into sales. I was so caught up in social media dogma that I was sure I knew everything about everything and was militant about it. All it took was one incredibly intelligent friend who used Socratic methods to ask me about my beliefs to make me understand that I really didn't know anything. That was earth-shattering for me and forced me to see the world through a sense of humility. That moment changed the rest of my life for the better.

Again, I had it happen when I started managing here and realized that I needed to actively read. Recently, I had it happen again. I had everything figured out. I was on this plateau of understanding where I could see everything so clearly and knew exactly how everything could be tweaked and changed for the betterment of the company. I was about to be unstoppable. However, I ran into an issue; I had to persuade managers in other departments to take on these ideas. Now, I'm thinking, who wouldn't take on these ideas? The benefits are as clear as day. However, no one wanted to test any of my ideas. I was frustrated. How could people not understand something that seems so simple, practical, and effective? My constant frustration from explaining, reexplaining, and getting nowhere wore me down and put me in a bad place.

One day, I was talking with Chad, who by this time had been promoted to the regional level. He told me my issue was that I was not good at communicating. Boy did that throw me for a loop. Am I not good at communicating? No one wants to hear that. I've always considered myself to be very good at teaching and explaining, but this is when I was told that if someone didn't take the same journey to reach my conclusion that they most likely would not understand that conclusion. If they haven't read the same books, watched the same podcasts, and gone through the same conversations, how could they arrive where I had? This meant I had to relearn how to communicate effectively. If I've ever felt a setback in my life, that was definitely it. That's a major change. However, if I commit to a change and adjust, that's an incredibly strong tool in my toolbox. Learning to communicate effectively with other management, as well as with my team, is an incredibly valuable leadership trait.

Every time you feel the floor taken out from under you, it's natural to get frustrated and angry. That is because we're confused. How could we be on top of the pinnacle in one moment and be back at the base of the mountain the next? To help with the confusion, understand that if this happens to you, you are going in the right direction.

In my experience, it's much better to teach through humility than through authority. I got my team to read books by opening up. I shared that, at first, I thought reading books didn't matter and then talked about my natural progression through reading. This will always work better than telling them they need to read books or asking why they aren't reading books. That doesn't work. You might as well be telling kids to clean their room. They're not going to want to. Treat your team like children, and you will have a room full of children. Remember that. If you treat your team like professionals, you will have a room full of professionals.

Say you're addressing a group of closers and you want them to spend more time warming up with customers. How many different ways can you explain to them how important it is to warm up with homeowners? You might get frustrated and start acting like they're idiots because you've been telling them to do it all year and they're not. Alternatively, perhaps you can tell them about when you started in sales. Tell them how you used to go through the pitch without using any warm-up or other basics. Tell them how hard that time was for you, how miserable you were. Then tell them about the shift in your thought process—how you took on warming up to customers and how that was the turning point in your career. Focus on that being the key to your success and you will have so many people following your lead because you showed them the clear path to success. Everyone wants—and needs—to see the clear path to success.

I know that humility is hard for some people to get behind. Besides, you got to your position because you put in the hours and the work. Naturally, we tend to lean toward a manner of authority when addressing a team. It also makes you feel like "the man" if you can speak from a point of authority. But ask yourself, does that get you closer to the goal? If you continuously come from a point of authority and your office stats aren't increasing, maybe it's time to look inward and see how you can bring something different to your team. Humility is a tool that will help your team buy in. Give it a shot. Even if it's somewhat uncomfortable, you'll get past that.

A leader will teach their team members to be as good or possibly better than themselves. If you are training someone to do your job, it is natural to teach how you do everything. That is good. It is a very good idea to clone yourself in the off chance that you have to leave your current position. However, you always want to expand on their strong suit and what's important to them as well. Keep in mind, none of us knows everything. Even if you are teaching someone who is less experienced, we can learn from them as well. If they are better than you in a certain area, don't be afraid to point it out. We can all be strong in most areas, so maybe that's something to work on; however, you may never even know that you're weak in an area until you recognize the strength of someone else.

In fact, this is one of the main reasons why I love the management course that I teach. This course is a great way for me to share my ideas and concepts while simultaneously using the team to help flesh them out. It's Hegelian dialectic. I bring the abstract, the team takes the concept through the negative, and we arrive at the concrete. I have many people in my class who have never held a management role anywhere; however, they constantly bring me ideas and concepts I had never considered. Teaching the management course is two-sided. I teach them fundamentals, and they teach me more esoteric perspectives.

As the office grows, you grow as well, and your team grows with you. It is always important to have a vision for yourself as well as the office. Have large future goals. Have yearly goals, monthly goals, and smaller goals. It's important to have office goals as well as personal goals to constantly bring you success. It may sound strange to have personal goals, but again, productivity is the name of the game whether that's in work or in life. If you are productive in one area, you will most likely increase your productivity in others.

For example, in 2021, my personal goals were to make $250,000, buy a house, buy another car, get back in shape, write a book, get promoted, and start on another kid. That is a fairly large year's worth of goals. However, as I'm writing this book, I'm fairly close to being on track for the yearly earnings goal, I'm closing on a house right now, and I've been working diligently at my job to get to the next level. The only part of this goal I haven't put an effort toward is going to the gym, though I'm going to have to. We need to hold ourselves accountable to the goals we set for ourselves. Success is our responsibility.

Being able to execute yearly goals like these will really propel your career forward. A lot of people get comfortable and coast. A leader can't afford to coast. If you coast, the team will coast until someone new shows you up and takes over.

While that's a good example of a yearly goal, let me show you an example of a personal future goal. First, however, it's important to have a strong motivation that moves you toward your future goal. Just like productivity is the office goal, if you find your personal goal, you can then ask if what you are doing is moving you in the direction of your personal goal.

A strong method to use when creating personal motivation is called "the why." When I first started here, I heard over and over again, "You need to find your why." It was explained as being the greatest reason behind where you are aiming in life that is always in the back of your mind, giving intent to every action you take.

Of course, like most things, I didn't buy in to the idea when I first heard it and didn't think of it as being that important. I heard it over and over again as time went on. People were touching on it vaguely, talking about the importance of it. One day, we had a guest speaker over a videoconference. It was a woman named Aparna, and she gave a powerful emotional story behind her "why." She talked about growing up in India, writing in her notebook by the light of the streetlamps, dreaming of one day making it to America. Her story was so powerful about where she came and where she was going and all her aspirations, and I finally understood why this method was so important.

So what's my "why"? Well, I grew up in a wealthy family. My grandfather was a millionaire and a huge part of the family. Upon his death, the money didn't last too long. My father took over my grandfather's excavation business, but he developed Parkinson's at an early age and couldn't keep it going. My mother and older brother are workaholics who have worked nine-to-fives their whole lives, but California is so expensive that it's hard to save much. Meanwhile, I married a woman from a poor family in a poor country that technically lives in an old, abandoned storefront. So my "why" was to move up the ranks in an expanding company with whom I will maintain my career. I want to move all of my family to this side of the country so we can be close again. I want to buy a new house for my wife's family and keep them financially stable, and I want to help my mother retire comfortably to the point that she never wants for anything again. This is a heavy goal that really puts pressure on me to grind and continue to grow. If you have your own significant "why" in the back of your head as you go out to work, you will be working with intent. You will work faster, longer, and in a way that people will want to work with you. Aparna said that she told her "why" to every customer she sat down with. That's a powerful message, and it's no wonder she has done so well.

Besides having powerful personal goals, it's important to help define and build personal goals for your team as well. Most individuals on a team are working solely for money or camaraderie. Not too many will actually have defined life goals. In fact, if you try to talk to them about life goals, most of them probably won't understand the benefits of simply writing them out. If you write something into existence, on some level you feel commitment to it.

If you put an effort into building a relationship with a team member, this will become much easier. As you understand them better, you can determine how far along in the process they are. Sometimes that can be enough to at least give people a perception of goals, even if they're short-term. Besides, most goals are something simple like buying a new car or even an expensive guitar.

Like I talked about my yearly goals earlier, you can ask your team about their New Year's resolutions. Most people don't stick to them, and they are widely mocked as a hallmark of the beginning to a new year. New year, new you, right? People have the same feeling about vision boards. I know I did. Yet after seeing that nearly everyone who's more successful than I am uses them, I'm a fool for mocking them. If you have successfully stuck to a yearly goal in the past and became more successful because of it, you can help your team perceive the opportunity therein. Of course, I use humility as the vehicle to take my team along that journey: "This is how I used to think ... this is the mental shift I had when I decided to start ... this is how my life was affected in the process ... this is how I think now ... this is how I apply to my life currently." It is a step-by-step plan for how to start using a powerful tool.

A lot of times, yearly goals seem overwhelming and out of reach, which is why so many people give up so easily. Again, they can't perceive the real opportunity there. So now it's our job to break it down into smaller increments. To make $100,000 a year seems like a lot of money. Do you think you can make $100,000?

If not, lets break that down per month. Do you think you can make $8,340 per month? That's $2,085 per week. Now it's starting to seem easier if they've made that much in a week before. That's approximately $350 per day. How much work do you need to do in order to make $350 per day? Let's say you need to have two appointments held. Okay, so what's your ratio of appointments set to appointments held? If that's 66 percent, then you need to acquire three appointments per day. How many conversations does it take for you to get one appointment? Let's say it's ten. How many doors do you need to knock on to get a conversation? Let's say it's five. So, that means you have to knock on 150 doors per day. Can you knock on 150 doors per day? That doesn't seem so hard. If that seems too hard, how about twenty-five doors per hour? It's exactly the same amount if you are working six hours. If you can break down a goal into the smallest timeframe, it's so much easier to perceive the opportunity that's in front of you. Not only that, if you're getting the three leads a day, each day will seem like a win. Now you have serotonin keeping you amped up, and if you're focused on the success in the shorter timeframes, you're going to be knocking on doors with quickness and intent. You will develop a habit that will push you consistently and change your life for the better.

Having office goals is absolutely a must. If you can get a team rallied behind an objective, your tribe will go to war for you. What is your vision for the office? How productive do you perceive it being one year out? Two years out? Five years out? Of course, you can share that vision with your team, but unless you're great at painting a vision, they probably won't see you as rational. Of course, it's sell or be sold to, so get used to selling your team on your vision or they will sell it back to you as a pipe dream.

If you can't sell your team on a five-year plan (you wouldn't need to anyway), break it down to yearly and monthly goals the same way I demonstrated for personal goals. When you break things down into smaller increments, everything seems so much more attainable. In fact, I like to do stretch goals—or, as I call them, moonshot goals. I like to aim for the upper realm of what we technically should be able to achieve if we were constantly firing on all cylinders. You will be surprised how much more productive you can be when you aim for a moonshot goal. Some managers and leaders like to aim for the lower realm of what the team can achieve so that they gain confidence when the office hits the goal. However, if your lower realm is 150 sales in a month, maybe you'll hit 160. But if you shoot for 200, maybe you'll hit 180. Why would anyone be defeated by that? As long as you are celebrating your team, they will be fine. Then it's back to work on an even higher goal!

Maybe you want to be competitive. In the first chapter, I talked about how we always chanted, "Beat Denver." That's something to rally behind. We did "Road to 200" to get us to achieve 200 sales. Maybe you're trying to break an office or company record. That's a goal to rally behind. Maybe you want your office to be the top-producing office in the company. That's a huge goal!

Of course, a big mistake I've seen offices make (including my own) is not replacing the goal when the original goal is complete. If you have fought for months to attain 200 sales in a month but you don't immediately replace it with "Road to 250," you are only incentivizing your team to relax. You made it. Game's over. That's a major mistake that will have a ton of opportunity cost. Of course, my office is currently comparing itself to entire states, and we are winning! I don't focus too much on that though. That's more for prestige than anything. My goal for this office is to be so incredibly dominant in our area of work that no other company can even find money here.

At the end of the last chapter, I talked about how an increase in opportunity doesn't equate to an increase in productivity. That is a hard idea to come to terms with. It is entirely counterintuitive. My job is literally to create opportunity. In fact, ever since I have been managing at this company, I have considered the setter side to be the opportunity side and the closer side to be the execution side. My team gets you in the door and you close the deal. I understand, however, that if I scale the office now with the glaring issues we have, the negative will be exponential. I have to change direction and refocus before we can even begin to think about scaling.

After checking in on how heavy hitters in the door-to-door industry do their work, it seems that farming neighborhoods is the natural progression of the door-to-door industry. Farming a neighborhood is when you stay within that neighborhood for one to three months, knocking on the same doors over and over again. What we've been doing is letting everyone go wherever they choose and, generally, each day we choose a neighborhood that hasn't been knocked on in about a month's time. The funny thing is that many times when you knock on a door, the homeowner will be upset and tell you that our company has knocked on their door five times and he's sick of it! Because of reactions like that, farming a neighborhood begins to feel counterintuitive. How would that person enjoy me knocking on their door once a week, let alone once a month?

That thought is just us projecting. In reality, people don't like their door knocked on by a *company*. If it is a different person knocking on their door once a month representing the same company, it's the equivalent to calling a service number and talking to a different person every time who has no idea of your particular situation. It's frustrating. However, if you call a service line and get the same representative who has a strong understanding of your specific situation, you are far more likely to perceive that company and that worker fondly. So shouldn't it be the same if it was the same person knocking on their door each time? They become familiar with you. They know you by name. They begin to talk and joke with you. Eventually, they won't even have a choice but to work with you.

In fact, I'm going to get a little weird here for a moment. While pondering these ideas, I began to think about virality of illnesses. For example, we get vaccinated so that illnesses can't simply spread through the population and thin out the herd. However, if you have a group of people who are vaccinated, yet one is not, if that one person is the carrier of the illness, something interesting happens. That illness will attempt to spread to other hosts but won't be able to survive there. However, the illness can survive on the original host body that hasn't been vaccinated. Therefore, the illness will try and try constantly as long as it's near the other bodies to find a way to the new host. Eventually, the illness can mutate to a new strain of itself that actually can survive on the new hosts. If that illness makes it to one, it has a significantly higher chance to move to another. The more hosts that it can inhabit, the higher the chance it has to spread.

Along the same lines, we have the word "meme," which generally refers to how specific behaviors can have a similar effect. It's like the virality of behavior. Say you have a group of well-mannered children who wouldn't dream of doing anything too wrong, yet you have one who wants to steal. At first, you can imagine the other kids think that stealing is a terrible idea and would never do something their parents have told them is an awful thing that only bad children do. They may even keep their distance from the troublemaker. However, if those children seem him playing with a brand-new toy and they're interested in that toy, they'll ask him where he got it. Well, he stole it. They could have one too if only they'd go with him. Or perhaps they could all steal toys on their own time and have a collection of awesome toys together. These well-mannered children may still resist; however, after enough time seeing all the cool toys this kid has, they have a much higher chance of reconsidering. If they begin to steal toys and never get caught, then it's safe to say that as they make more friends, those friends will probably take on similar traits.

Couldn't the same be said for knocking on doors? If you have a neighborhood with no solar panels and the homeowners haven't heard anything about solar, they probably won't be interested. However, if you have one install on a street, the rest of the street is now at least curious and far more likely to receive information about how solar can benefit their home.

What if there are two installs on the same street? Well now that percentage goes up even higher! What if you are the only person they ever see? What if everyone on the street knows you by name as the solar guy? Well if they all of a sudden have a curiosity in solar, doesn't that make you the guy to talk to? After you have four or five installs on one street, do you think these families who like you may refer their friends and family to you? Now you have new neighborhoods to farm!

It seems to me that this is the natural evolution of the door-to-door game, and while my office is thriving right now, if there is ever a better path, you should always be open to exploring the better path. If you are a leader, not just a manager, your team will follow you wherever you take them. Like farming is the natural progression of knocking on doors, the leader is the natural progression of the manager.

Become a leader. Never settle for just being a manager.

Culture

A good culture is the most powerful asset you can have in an office environment. Far too often we hear that people hate their jobs and their bosses. We hear about bosses managing with fear, using anything they can to make sure workers know their place. If you manage this way, you will not gain loyalty or have nearly as much production. People want to work. Our biggest mistake is micromanagement and leading with fear. If we simply create and maintain a good culture and get out of people's way, they will do what they came to your office to do: work. You may single-handedly be holding your team back if you do not understand this.

Of course, I use personal growth as an ethos throughout my office. The interesting thing is that many companies already have a culture. It may even be a fantastic culture, but sometimes the managers of individual offices either don't realize it or don't know how to tap into it. In fact, I didn't realize that the ethos of the company I work for is personal growth. My bosses were definitely interested in my personal growth both inside and outside the office, but I didn't understand that this concept went to the top of the company. The moment that my co-manager and I developed a strong culture within our office, I was incredibly proud of what we had created. However, looking back now, I'm not entirely sure whether that was the natural development from a company with that particular culture trickling down from the top or we simply replicated it on our own. Either way, it does take the office managers to implement a culture. When we did, the difference in our office was like the difference between night and day.

Earlier in the book, I described an issue that our office had. We had a highly productive setter who was challenging everything that Justin and I did as managers. This setter believed that he had a better way of managing and he attempted to change things within the office, even going as far as attempting to recruit other setters to create a counterculture. Every time we attempted to sit down with this individual and ask him to dial it back, he was unwilling to do so. As much as we were upset with this individual, he was a product of our lack of culture. It really was our fault, although we didn't see it that way.

We decided to part ways with this individual. He was, at the time, someone we couldn't work with. He was creating a division within the office. In fact, we had some veterans and heavy hitters who didn't want to even set foot in the office and deal with that individual.

But again, the real issue was not the individual. Justin and I had very little respect from our team. Because of this, the team came to meetings late. They worked when they wanted to. Some didn't even work, they came to meetings just to hang out. That pissed off the people who were serious, and they interpreted those actions as a lack of management. Even during our meetings, setters were interrupting us with jokes, trying to speed us up, and being incredibly disrespectful.

With the understanding that the lack of respect from our team was directly associated with having no minimum standards in our office, we decided to implement an accountability structure. When it comes to discipline, you always want to do that in private. When you discipline in private, the one getting disciplined will tell their team anyway and that discipline will spread throughout the team. Everyone will get the message.

We decided to create a clear metric. If you fell below this metric on a weekly basis, we would bring you into a one-on-one meeting in the office. We would first ask why this setter thought their production was so low and if there was anything we could do to help. We wanted to show that we were looking out for their best interests and we were there to help. Of course, we understood that, most of the time, the issue would simply be that they weren't working very much. Most people told us that. If it was, in fact, because they were not working enough, we put them on a three-week probationary period. We gave them a minimum standard to hit, and they needed to work toward that goal every week. The moment they hit the goal, they were off the probationary period. However, if they weren't working toward the goal, we would sit back down with them the next week and talk them through it. And if they didn't reach the goal in three weeks, we would part ways with them. They clearly weren't interested in being a productive part of the team.

The moment that we not only implemented but enforced this structure, it greatly changed how our office was acting. Everyone began coming to the meetings. They were on time. They were paying attention. They went out and worked. Our productivity went up and became consistent! This simple structure provided a huge benefit for what we were trying to create.

Having this accountability structure was the initial foundation that allowed us to begin working on our culture. Accountability is not something you want to focus on. That is where most offices and managers lose. When everything is about accountability, everyone works out of fear of losing something. Again, that won't create loyalty. Accountability is something that should be a reality but not a focus. Having it be a policy that is simply there will allow the management to be the inspiration. If you do this correctly, you will have people inspired by you but the onus will be on them if they are not productive. That puts you in the best possible position for your team. You want to bring the positivity to your office.

The best thing about the setup of our office was that we had an incredible individual who we weren't utilizing properly. Justin had been managing the team all year long, but he never had creative control over his job. Of course, creative control is something I demanded the moment I became his co-manager, and I soon realized that he had been working without it. If you take creativity away from a motivator, you put that person in a box and they will not buy in to their job. The accountability structure was Justin's idea. He knew how to gain the respect of his team, and we campaigned to implement the idea in our office. The moment that it worked exactly how it was designed to work, I saw a completely new Justin. He became the highly energetic and enthusiastic motivator and is now a rock star in our company. He can bring the passion and positivity to the office every time he walks in the door. This is an invaluable skill.

Again, the definition of sales is the transference of believe from you to the customer. This is also true from the management to the team. Now that Justin is enthusiastic about what we do, he hands that enthusiasm to the team. It's the same thing if you come in stressed; you will only hand that stress to the team. It's the same thing if you are defeated, desperate, or uncertain. You will only hand those things over to the team. The same thing is true from the setter or closer team to their customers. If they are stressed or desperate, every customer can feel that and they will have a hard time earning any accounts. That stress or desperation might be tracked all the way back to the management during meetings. It's our job to give our teams positivity and confidence so that they can carry that into their day-to-day. We have a much bigger influence on our team than we realize.

A word of warning—Don't manufacture this. If you are going to bring motivation to your team, you must have heart. You have to be willing to bring this to a real emotional level. I have seen managers try to pump up their team with theatrics. Theatrics work a lot like an internet video. You might get people psyched up for an hour—if they don't feel embarrassed for you. But if you make it real and authentic, you will own the room.

When it comes to creating a culture, this is where a manager is really challenged. This is when a manager has to look deep within themselves and ask if they are the right person to lead the team. A manager deals with the day-to-day and the running of the office. They make sure everything is afloat and not in decline. There is, however, a sizable difference between being a manager and being a leader.

A leader is someone everyone looks up to. A leader is someone people not only want to work for but want to fight for. A leader doesn't make sure they keep everyone in check. Instead, a leader builds everyone up and shows them the way forward. A leader has everyone's best interest at heart and cares about the individual in both their work and home life. People don't buy into managers; they buy into, trust, and respect leaders.

Remember when I said companies want managers who lead from the front? That's because if the manager is in the trenches, doing the hard work with the team, and setting a strong example, the team will naturally see them as their leader. It is the "easy" path to gaining leadership. I say easy when it really isn't, but the reason it's coveted by corporate is because they can measure it through statistics. It's hard to measure any other way.

In my experience, the best way to gain leadership is through vulnerability. Unfortunately, this idea is counterintuitive to most people who have worked hard enough to gain management. Why would I be vulnerable? Shouldn't I tell them about all the crazy work and effort that I put in to get to where I am? Oh, you definitely can—and should. However, if you are bragging about your past adventures, does that get people to buy in to you? Doesn't that make you just like a bad boss that you see in movies? You laugh at the absurdity when you see that boss portrayed on TV, but it is our natural go-to as humans. We love to gloat. We love admiration. Is talking to your team in this manner taking your team closer to the goal? Is it building them up?

Let me give you an example of teaching from status versus teaching from a state of vulnerability.

My company wants everyone to read books. We have a book of the month that is generally sales-related or self-help. It's a fantastic policy that I thoroughly enjoy, though I didn't always feel that way. In fact, I never read books before I joined this company. I was also fairly set against reading these books. However, now it is a part of my job to get as many people on the team to read these books as I can.

Persuading people to read books from a point of status looks a little bit like this: "Our book of the month is *Greenlights* by Matthew McConaughey. Who here plans on reading it? Guys! You all have time to read this book. You all have a half an hour you can take out of your TV time to put toward this. It's going to help you. I read five books a month and manage you guys. You all can read one. If you try to tell me you don't have time, that's absolute BS."

Sound familiar? Nearly everywhere I've worked, that's how my bosses have been.

Now this is what getting this message across looks like through a state of vulnerability: "Our book of the month is *Greenlights* by Matthew McConaughey. Who here is going to read it? You know, when I started working here, I never read books. I was pretty hard set against it actually. Upper management kept pushing the idea to me until I finally gave in and started reading. Once I started reading a book a month, it wasn't long before I began reading two books a month, then three. My perspective has never changed so fast so often in my entire life. I'm sure you all can tell that the person I was even three months ago is different than who I am today. That's simply because I've been reading. It's not only changing the way I interact with you here at work, but it's changed the way I think and interact with my home life. My relationship with my wife is better. My relationship with my family is better. I am more productive and happier. Reading has been the best investment I have ever made in myself, and I want the same for every one of you."

Quite a difference, right? Nearly my entire team reads the book of the month every month and some read multiple books. In fact, I'm running a management course that I call "Future Leaders." Everyone in that course has a second book to read every month.

If you were going to read a book, which manager do you think would have a better shot of persuading you?

This method also goes back to the perception of opportunity. Most people refuse to try anything if they can't understand how it will benefit them. If you have personally come to a conclusion based on the things that you've done, the route that you took, the books that you read, the podcasts that you've watched, try and hand that conclusion to someone and notice they will not agree or even try to understand it. That's because they didn't take the same journey as you. They can look at a conclusion and not have any perception of opportunity with the route you have given them. If you only say, "Please read books! It will help you," they won't understand how reading books can help them.

Through vulnerability, you can open up about when you were on their level. This is incredibly important. You have to meet them where they are currently at. You come down to their level of understanding, show them the path you've taken, and be real and open about the changes you have made in the process. This shows them a direct route to opportunity, and they will be far more likely to take that route.

I also never tell anyone that I'm better than they are at what I do. I may be better at this point in my journey, but we are all on a journey. Some just started earlier or went faster than others. One person from upper management often says, "I'm only as good as I am because I have failed more times than you have."

That's powerful, and it also reveals a route to opportunity. Failing shouldn't be held in negative regard. Failing is a very important element throughout life. We learn through failure. We grow through failure. We should never feel defeated in failure. We should be proud of the experience we are collecting in order to move away from failure. You want to be great? You have to fail. You may have to fail a lot. But you keep going, you learn, and you grow.

Vulnerability will earn the respect and trust of your team. It makes you human, but it's a level that is uncomfortable for most. I find vulnerability to be more powerful than only leading from the front because your team will start coming to you often for advice even outside of work. If you can get your team to buy in to you on a bigger scale than work, they will want the best for you. When your leadership style is just by leading from the front, you are more likely to have someone challenge you in an attempt to take your place.

That being said, if you do not actively read books or learn in some capacity, you probably don't have a lot that you can teach. I said before that I realized very quickly I had an empty well to draw from, and reading was how I was going to fill that well. Reading multiple books every month will give you so much material to work with. Every week will involve new teachings, and you can bring the takeaways to your team. Your team will grow with you and view you as irreplaceable.

Culture, of course, isn't solely based on reading, although reading is a huge foundation to build from. You should constantly be promoting personal growth because if the members of your team are growing as people, they will love the place they work.

It's also important to inspire your team. If you can bring the motivation of a YouTube motivational video to your team by yourself—and on a real level—it will be hard for them not to be inspired. That's an attribute that will get your team motivated! Inspire your team to be more, to be better, to contribute to something greater than themselves! Let them know this isn't just a job; this is a career that's going to take them where they want to go in life. Encourage them to have bigger life goals, and help them get there. A house? A new car? A family? Show them how to get there and how the company is the vehicle to get them wherever they want to go in life.

The way we talk about the job will change the culture. Are we telling people to sell? Or are we telling people to help and provide service? Even when our closers close a deal, they don't post that they "closed." Every new contract is posted with the word "helped." We aren't closing them; we are helping them. If we stick to that concept in the office away from the customers, it's only natural for the idea to bleed into the rest of the job. When we are knocking on doors, we need to be talking to potential customers from the stance of having their best interest at heart. If you become an office that is known for service, you will become popular fast.

It is also important to care about the individual. Justin and I give everything we have to our team. Honestly, there are a lot of times I'm not even sure that we're doing the right thing in the moment. However, seeing the results afterward always reinforces the importance of how far you may need to go to care for an individual. Sometimes a person's production with fall off. Everyone is human, and everyone has something going on. Sometimes we forget about that because, for managers, work is life. But to other people, life is life. Many times people go through breakups that mess them up. Sometimes a family member dies. Sometimes people get sick. Sometimes people get in trouble and end up in jail. Sometimes people struggle with substance abuse. We've dealt with these and far worse. Every time, we are there for our team members. We give them anything they need. We give our time, our advice, our help, and our money. We give so much care that it shows how much we value our team. When people feel valued, they buy in. They come back. They become examples for everyone else. The best part is, they will show the same care to the rest of our team. Our team cares about each other and wants the best for each other. This, of course, makes our jobs easier.

It is important to have office goals as well. You always want something that the team can aspire to achieve. Every individual can contribute to the office goal. For us, it used to be 200 contracts in a month. Now we have a few different goals. We want 250 contracts in a month. We want our one office in Virginia Beach to be more productive than all the combined offices in the state of Texas (which currently we are). And we want to be so dominant in the Hampton Roads area that no other company can even find money here. We want to operate on such a high level that there is no point for anyone else to even attempt to do business here. We are going for the throat! That contributes to the culture! As management, we have a dominant mindset, and so does the rest of the team.

We are dominant. We are here to serve. We want the best for each other. We grow together. We thrive together. We die together. That is a cultural bond that is far beyond any office that I have ever been a part of. You want a shot at being great? You have to value and build relationships with your team.

The idea of leading from the front is a strong idea. Of course, I have redefined the meaning of lead from the front in this book. Whereas the industry wants it to mean that you do the job that you are managing on a much more productive level than your team, I believe that leading from the front is being productive on a higher level than your team in anything that pushes your office toward the goal. After all, the goal is office productivity. Do your personal stats take precedence over all the other things you could be doing to make your office productive? It's incredibly difficult to justify that. Either way, you earn the same respect and trust from your team with both methods. The difference is that if your metric is productivity, you can do far more to benefit the office.

The greatest downfall of the original "lead from the front" method is that if you build your entire culture around it, you are going to run into a few inevitable issues. If your personal production defines your management, you will incentivize your heavy hitters to challenge you. And if they can outproduce you, why shouldn't they be the managers instead?

More importantly, if your culture is "lead from the front" culture, what happens if you get sick or go on vacation? Well, if the example burns out, the office stops working. You may think this sounds crazy, but I watch it happen again and again to the point that I can call it out before it happens.

It blows my mind that with all of the negative sides to this culture method, companies still preach it as gospel instead of trying to expand on it or find something better.

We refer to the culture that our office has created as "buy-in" culture. Are you bought in? Are you bought in to me? Are you bought in to the job? Are you bought in to the goals? Are you bought in to the direction? Are you bought in to the company? Are you bought in to yourself?

So, what does "buy-in" even mean?

Buying in doesn't happen overnight. It takes time, but the success that comes once it does happen is overwhelming. It starts with the process. If you are naive enough to trust the process—or curious enough to follow the process—you will quickly find yourself part of something bigger than a job. The process starts with personal growth. Can you buy in to me as a leader? Can you buy in to where I'm taking you? Is this simply a job or is this the career that is going to change your entire life? Is this the career that is going to get you everything you've always wanted? If so, are you going to do everything that it takes to get there? Are you going to do what you have to do? Are you going to find a way no matter what?

If you are truly bought in to this, are you going to give it everything you've got when it's raining? Are you going to give it everything you've got when it's snowing? In the dark? In the morning? Are you going to work the hours? Are you going to learn and grow with us? Are you going to follow the company as it evolves and changes? Are you bought in to being a part of something bigger than anything that you've been a part of before?

If you are really bought in, you are going to give every bit of what you have to this. And we are going to give every bit of what we have to you.

Are you bought in to our instruction? Are you actively reading to improve yourself? Are you giving everything that you have to the team? Are you caring about their well-being?

Does this sound like a cult yet?

Actually, we hear that a lot. The truth is that when you are bought in to what we do here and you follow the process and you give it everything you have, you will greatly see your quality of life increase. I get texts and calls all the time from members of my team thanking me for what we've done. Some tell me they started going to the gym and are losing weight. Some give up vices like smoking. Some begin taking real steps toward healing relationships with their families and friends. Many people who start being productive in their own lives begin to see that everything is achievable. Nothing is too far out of anyone's reach if you simply make a conscious effort to make it happen. They begin to understand that productivity is the name of the game—not just at work but in life in general.

To be honest, that is exactly how it worked for me. When I was in high school, I wanted to be a writer. Then I realized how little most authors make in terms of money, so I decided to go in different directions. All my life I wanted to write a book but never thought that I could or that anyone would even want to read it. After I made a commitment to read five books a month, I started seeing everything differently. My perspectives on many things have changed in a very short amount of time, and I have constantly been increasing my productivity. Recently, it hit me that I needed to write a book. I knew I was onto something important and have learned that if you feel that way about something, you need to aim for it. I didn't have a choice but to write this book. The moment I sat down to start writing, I realized how realistic it is for anyone to write a book. The hardest part is simply sitting down and starting.

With buy-in culture, the members of my team are constantly growing as people. They are becoming smarter. They are becoming more empathetic. They are working out the issues in their own lives and becoming better people. That bleeds into their work. It's an infinite game. It's a constant progression. Once my team members started understanding how much potential they have, many of them started seeing themselves as having the potential to become leaders. Many have actually come to me about learning the management side.

Recently, I have started a management class that teaches the mechanics and theory of management, as well as having some workshop items. My normal setter team has approximately thirty-five setters and fifteen of those are in my management course. At first, I thought that the number would die down after a couple of weeks, but I have maintained every person in that class as well continue to add members.

I am not afraid of having anyone learn my job. I am not afraid to lose my job. In fact, I used to believe that my value came from how proficient I am at my job; however, lately (through reading) I have come to understand that I can scale my value with the amount of people I impact. If I teach people how to do my job well, that's fantastic. They can take my job. I have shown a value even greater than my job. This is why you see artists and teachers turn to social media use when they realize that they have something special. You can either teach a class or you can teach the world.

Which do you think is more sustainable? "Lead from the front" culture or buy-in culture? One of the best attributes of buy-in culture is that the office never declines and never has off months. It is incredibly consistent, and will continue to be month after month and, theoretically, year after year.

You may be reading this and think that this method is too uncomfortable. Well, get comfortable being uncomfortable. If you ever feel uncomfortable about something that will bring you success, that is the direction to go. If you become comfortable with it, you will add a tool to your toolbox.

Now that we have this culture, almost every single person who joins our team is referred to us by a current employee. Our team is excited to show everyone how much money they can make and what kind of team they can be a part of. When we have new people join, even rough-around-the-edges, career salesmen, they are blown away by our culture and say that they've never worked anywhere else like it. They want to be a part of it. They want to contribute to it.

In fact, it's gotten to the point where even toxic individuals who come in don't have the room to be toxic. They will become less toxic in order to fit into the team. This is the one thing that I've thought about a lot over the last few months. The individual who we fired would not have been an issue within our current culture. It was our lack of culture that allowed him to act that way.

If he was to come into our office today, he would only be a highly productive and contributing part of the team. As hard as it is to see these things when they're happening, it's important to know when our methods and policies are letting our team down.

I do believe that culture has had the biggest impact on our setter team. If you don't think culture is important, believe it. If you have never thought about the culture in your office, pay attention to how you speak to your team. Pay attention to how they respond and react to you. There is a good chance that you could use some unification. If you are looking to change the culture, first figure out whether your company already has a good culture from the top. Again, many people don't even realize that there is an ethos in place you can simply tap into. That makes it so much easier because you don't have to define anything. It's already present. You can just be the leader who brings it to the team.

But if you have to create the culture from the ground up, imagine how that will look to upper management. If you can successfully bring a culture to your office when the company has never explored culture, you will have a good shot at finding your way to the top of that company.

Always make sure that you are consistently the right leader to bring your team along the company's progression.

Chapter 12:

The Autonomous System

As you may have gathered by this point in the book, I have a desire to pick apart policies and systems already in place. That, of course, doesn't make the me the most popular person in my place of work, especially at first.

If you are trying to create, recreate, or expand upon policies, systems, and structures, you have to be decent at selling your ideas to your team. You can't just tell them, "There's a new system; let's implement it and it will work better." No one is going to get behind that. I have definitely learned how important it is to have data and statistics, along with being incredibly patient with the team. It's a requirement if you want to implement nearly anything new that you use the power of perception to bring them along. Not everyone is going to have a real understanding of how a policy is actually working. Most people just have an understanding of what it's meant to affect. Again, I'm not interested in what is *supposed* to work. I'm only interested in what *actually* works. So, sometimes we have to pick apart existing processes and see how and if they're contributing to the goal. We take data and see how that policy could be altered in order to increase production. Once you have that data, along with a better way of doing something, present it to your team. Now they can follow your line of thinking. If they can't perceive the opportunity within the new structure, they won't buy in. That's not their fault—that's yours. It means you have to do a better job bringing ideas up in the future with even more data and statistics until they can see the direction it could take them.

Throughout the time I've spend managing at ION Solar, I've collected a lot of data and statistics. Considering all the different aspects of managing a door-to-door team, I was looking for the ability to implement a series of policies that would have the office constantly moving toward the goal in every capacity before even having to manage. If there were policies that were simply in place that had the ability to corral cats, that would free up the rest of us to work on other things. In order to execute a system like this, there's a few things that would need to be implemented based on the data I've maintained.

First, of course, the policies are completely worthless unless they are steering the team toward the goal. That is a must. In fact, considering it's a system of policies that directs people toward the goal, the policies need to have a strong synergy so that we don't end up with loopholes or stagnation. These policies need to provoke constant motion.

Next, we need to implement policies that account for those driven by success and gain as well as those driven by fear of loss. Keep in mind, it's not entirely a negative thing when someone is driven by fear of loss. Managers just need to be conscious of it and use their motivation to push those people toward the goal.

Also, we need to use all methods of compensation within the office environment: money, status, and the perception of opportunity. In fact, I see the perception of opportunity being the most important factor to have in these policies. The team needs to be able to perceive what is actually achievable for them to accomplish.

Lastly, we must have these policies bring a stronger sense of self-determination to the offices. Most people take a 1099 position with commission because they are sick of a nine-to-five with an hourly rate while being micromanaged by their bosses. One of the main reasons people try out this industry is because they want to experience self-determination. People are sick of being told when to work, how to work, and how much they are worth. If we can make a system that rewards people for their self-determination, they will be much more likely to continue self-improvement as well as shoot for higher goals.

In this chapter, I'm going to break down a system of policies that my office has put in place that is specifically designed to have the office constantly moving toward the goal. Of course, keep in mind that the structure in every office is different; however, I do believe that this idea can be replicated with many different variations.

My office has a few different aspects. We have setters who knock on doors and set appointments. We have "self-gen," who knock on doors and close their own appointments. Then we have closers who run and close appointments that have already been set. And we have managers who, of course, manage. We want to incorporate all aspects of the office to make this as effective as possible.

The first policy we want to implement is the groundwork for accountability on the setter side. Sometimes, people join the company as a setter, yet all they want to do is come to meetings and hang out. Sometimes they never even work. That's just a waste of space for us. We need to have setters hold themselves accountable for the work they do and goals they create. That's why we implemented a minimum standard of work anyone should be able to do as long as they are working. Otherwise, misery loves camaraderie. If people just join to hang out, other setters will begin slacking as well. We can't have that. In fact, we want the opposite. We want the hardworking setters to rub off on the lost ones and bring them up. That's definitely something that will happen if the culture is strong. However, an accountability structure is meant to provide a minimum standard by feeding the fear of loss.

The accountability structure is generally for people who are new and haven't been improving or for setters who are either slacking off or going through a fairly long dry spell. If a setter is brand-new, we don't expect them to be great at their job. We expect them to be improving. If they aren't improving over a certain period of time, we first have to determine whether we have done a disservice to this setter by not giving them all the tools and attention they need. Remember, as leaders, it's always important to look inward first. That's how we learn and become better leaders.

Whether it's a newer setter who hasn't improved or an active setter who is going through a dry spell, we deal with them the same exact way. We hold a one-on-one meeting in the office. We have their stats pulled up so that when we sit down, we can let them know what the expectation is and where they are. This immediately makes the conversation a serious one. We need to have their attention. Then the first question we ask is, "Is there anything that we can provide you with or help you with in order to help you achieve the standard?" This is important. This question serves a couple of ends. The first thing it does is let the setter know that we are looking out for their best interest. Normally, a tough conversation with management ends with the setter simply feeling like a tool for a machine who can easily be replaced. We don't want anyone to feel that way. We whole-heartedly want to help them reach and increase their potential.

The other thing that asking that question does is separate the management from the policy. That way, the setter doesn't feel like accountability is the focus of the management; it's simply a reality within the office that everyone abides by. Personally, I don't want fear of loss to be a focus in the office at all. People need to be motivated by it, of course, but the office environment is so much better if the accountability is just a reality. If we are detached from it as managers, it frees us up to be the constant positivity and inspiration that we want the team to focus on.

When we ask that question, generally we get the same response: the setter hasn't been putting in the work. If the case is, in fact, that the setter isn't working the hours, there's not much help that we can give them. Because of this, the onus is entirely on the setter. In the case that the issue is that the setter isn't working enough, we put them on a three-week plan. We remind the setter of the minimum standard they must hit in order to stay working here. The standard is a certain amount of weekly productivity. Because it's weekly productivity, we let the setter know that if they don't hit the minimum standard this week, we will be sitting down with them to have the same conversation next week. During that conversation, we will again ask how we can help them and then move on to the new week. If the setter doesn't hit the minimum standard the next week, we will sit down one last time and let them know that if they can't hit the minimum standard over one more week, we will have to part company with them.

Normally if the issue is that the setter hasn't been working the hours, they will do what they need to do the next week in order to be taken off the plan. However, we need to stay true to our systems. If the setter is unwilling to improve or to be as productive as what is required, we must part company. While firing someone may technically seem like a negative thing, ultimately, they fired themselves. The benefit that comes from their departure is that they can no longer bring down the team with their bad habits. Also, once the team realizes that a member is gone, they become more motivated to work.

The other accountability procedure that we use is that at the beginning of every week, we have the team tell us their weekly goals. We write these weekly goals on a large whiteboard. Then at the beginning of the next week, we revisit what they posted and how productive they actually were. When we originally ask for their goals, managers write the goals on the board. However, when it's time to show their productivity, we have the setter write what they did on the board next to their goal. If they are at the goal or over, we give them a blue marker. If they are under, we give them a red one. This will makes individual setters more attached to their goals in the future. If they are below their original weekly goal, we ask them what we can do as managers to help them attain their goals. It's the same question we use for the three-week plan. We want our team to know that we are here to help them get where they want to go. Remember, we don't want to stifle our team. The last thing we want to do is tell them to aim lower because it's more achievable. It's our job as leaders to bring them to the level they want to be.

The second part of the autonomous system is having "team leads." In our office, a team lead is a temporary position for the top four performers over a two-week span. Basically, every two weeks, we take the top four producers and have them be team captains for a snake draft. The captains draft all the other setters in the office into four teams. Then over a two-week period, if their team reaches a certain level of productivity, the captain earns a bonus of $500.

I know I reviewed the creation of the team lead position early in this book; however, originally, the position was created to promote camaraderie. We originally wanted the heavy hitters inviting the rest of the team to work during the pandemic. However, if you look at the position itself, it addresses all three forms of compensation.

First, the team lead position is based on status. It highlights who was the most productive over a two-week period. This is incredibly uplifting to the people who really put in the extra effort and shows them that they are not being overlooked. When the captain chooses their team, you can see how invested in the captain's role they get. Their self-confidence and self-determination skyrocket.

Second, they have a chance to earn an extra $500. That may not seem like a lot of money to some people; however, they do get very creative. When we first rolled this out, the captains were promising a cut of the prize to each teammate. Some would give a cut to the top producers on the team. Now, we're seeing that whenever a team wins, the captain will use the $500 to take the team out to an awesome day of golfing or nice restaurants. The team captains really start building up the culture within the office, which is invaluable.

Third, the team lead position provides a strong perception of opportunity. When the rest of the setters see one of their friends become a team lead, they see what it takes to achieve that and can see the clear path to becoming a team lead. Also, considering the team lead changes every two weeks, literally everyone has an opportunity to shoot for it. There is no tenure or favoritism. It is simply based on the work. Now, if the setter is self-determined enough, they can also become a team captain and enjoy that status and potential pay.

What's interesting about the perception of opportunity as it pertains to a team lead is that, originally, I thought it would only provide perception to the rest of the setter team. However, it turns out that whenever a setter becomes a team lead, they gain a new perception seeing the opportunity to move up. When a setter becomes a team lead, they being to think that if they can reach the top of their team, maybe they can become a self-gen. Maybe they can become a closer. Or, if that's not what their vision is, they may start believing that they can go into management. After a setter becomes a team lead, we notice them working more consistently and becoming more productive because they can now perceive so much more opportunity within the office.

Having a policy in the office that contains all three methods of compensation has been a fantastic asset to the environment.

The third aspect of the autonomous system is to have clear metrics for people to move into new roles. One of the biggest frustrations I've ever had with a company was with ION when I was trying to move into new roles myself. Because I was ever only given vague expressions instead of metrics to hit, I was confused. The natural response to confusion is frustration and anger. When we have a process that is designed to create frustration and anger, that doesn't create a good environment. In fact, if there are no clear metrics for moving from one position to the next, your team will most likely see promotions as forms of favoritism or nepotism. Whether that is the case or not, it creates an even worse environment.

Implementing clear metrics promotes self-direction and takes the onus completely off management. Now the onus is on the individual—where it should be. Also, having clear metrics provokes the perception of opportunity even further. If the team knows what they need to do in order to go where they'd like to go, they are far more likely to work toward that goal. They will also see that their efforts aren't in vain. Of course, we do pay people, but most people long for more than just money. People also long for fulfillment. If they can perceive their efforts as also working toward a personal goal, their work becomes more meaningful.

The first set of metrics we set were for the setters to become self-gen. In our office, in order for a setter to become self-gen, they need to have a certain high standard of productivity two weeks in a row. If they can become consistent in that high level of productivity, we give them the option of moving over. The goal that we identified is not easy to hit even for one week, so in order for someone to hit it two weeks in a row, they need to be very determined. Of course, once they accomplish it, they are free to move up or stay as a setter. While most people may read this and be confused about why someone would like to stay a setter, we do pay them very well. Also, being a setter and being a salesperson are two completely different skill sets with two completely different learning curves. Just because someone is a good setter does not mean they will be a good salesperson. We make it very clear to everyone who wants to move up that they shouldn't beat themselves up if they don't find success in sales. They can always move back to being a setter where they thrived and made good money. Besides, they can always try again in the future if they'd like.

Because of this particular setup of clear metrics, when someone gets promoted, the team no longer looks at the situation as unfair. Instead, the team will celebrate the promotion of someone who clearly deserves it. The funny thing is that most offices wouldn't want to lose their top setters for fear of lack of production in that department. Many places will attempt to keep strong setters in their department as long as possible.

The way I see it, if we hold down the top producers and promote setters who aren't as stellar, we are only teaching our team to be average. That means we will only reinforce our decision in holding on to the high producers because technically we are teaching the rest of the team to work less anyway. However, if we promote our top producers, we are revealing a clear path through excellence. Every time we have promoted a top producer, other setters have stepped up to take their place immediately and the rest of the team becomes even more productive.

In fact, setters taking over the spot when the heavy hitters leave is a phenomenon that's found in nature. You can see similar behavior in orangutans. If you've ever seen a large male orangutan with a wide flattened face, that is a dominant male. Within a group of orangutans, a dominant male will become fairly large and develop what's called a flange. The flange is what contributes to the shape of the face and its size is determined by the ape's level of testosterone. The orangutans get so large that they tend to stay on the ground rather than the trees. The females will come to the dominant male to mate while the other male orangutans will have to rely on methods such as rape for procreation.

The interesting thing about the orangutan is that as long as there is a dominant male filled with testosterone, the other males will remain in a juvenile state, regardless of their age. When the dominant males pass away, there won't be such a high level of testosterone to compete with and another male will grow in size, gain more testosterone, and develop a flange, making it the next dominant male.

Along the same lines, when there is a setter who is so incredibly dominant and consistent that they are constantly at the top of the leaderboards for productivity, others who would like to be at the top may not be able to see how their efforts could top that individual. Because of this, they are less likely to even try, whether they can top it or not. However, once that dominant setter moves on, there is a space to be filled. Someone will fill that space and sometimes even be more productive than the last setter.

Another hallmark of having setters move to the self-gen stage through excellence is that it will instill in the mind of that setter that they need to continue being excellent. Setters should be under the understanding that when they move on, they should expect to keep up high levels of work and production.

A self-gens job is to knock on doors, set appointments for themselves, and close their own deals. They are the epitome of door-to-door salespeople. The compensation jump moving from being a setter to a self-gen is fairly large, and there is more work involved having to learn how to be proficient at both jobs.

Again, this is where I had the most frustration within the office. When I was a self-gen, I was trying to become a closer. No matter how many deals I closed or how much of a role model I was, management wouldn't give me the opportunity to be a closer. Then a self-gen who did less work got promoted before me. That, of course, only made me think that the systems are based on favoritism or simply that management didn't really like me at the time. That is a problem that can easily be solved with clear metrics.

For moving from self-gen to closer, we implemented a certain level of production that must be done in a month's time to demonstrate a certain amount of effort and a high level of execution that is needed to take care of the leads who are handed to closers. This is because the setters' pay is now in the hands of the closers. We can't just have anyone running these appointments if they are not going to take care of them. Therefore, for a self-gen to become a closer, they need to demonstrate the consistent excellence required so that we know that they are giving their best to every lead they receive.

If the self-gen can see the clear metrics to the next level, they are far more likely to work harder and become more proficient faster in order to move to the next position. Again, this is using the perception of opportunity. In fact, ever since we instituted clear metrics to move into the closer role, we have not been able to keep people in the self-gen position for very long.

The fourth aspect of the autonomous system is having an accountability system for the closer side. Of course, no one makes it to the closer side unless they show that they are consistently productive and have earned it every step of the way. We have an incredibly strong team of closers. However, if you create a rigorous system in order to get to the top, managers become reluctant to hold them accountable if they start slipping. We know what they have gone through in order to get to where they are today. This brings up one very negative aspect to being a closer: they now have tenure.

Tenure is when a position has been earned and there is no way to lose that position. It is theirs as long as they choose to be there. While people would look at the closer role and wonder why someone would squander a position that gives them access to so much earning potential and prestige, you have to understand how easy it can be to become complacent in a role like this.

First off, not everyone understands the concept of money. In fact, I would say that most people don't. If someone is used to making $2,000 a month and gets a job with a higher earning potential, they typically make $2,000 in one week and then slack off for the rest of the month. This sounds crazy, but it happens everywhere. It's our job as leaders to help our team understand the concept of money by creating and attaining goals or helping them construct grander visions. We need to help them see how much they can actually achieve in their lives.

Second, people try incredibly hard to become good at the job while they are self-gen. However, once they become a closer, they are handed three to four leads to run per day that they didn't have to knock on doors for. If they are consistently making fantastic money, more than they could've ever imagined, it's only natural for them to begin cutting corners and not take their time executing these appointments very well. This will end with the closer only closing the low-hanging fruit and letting nearly anything that takes even a little bit of effort go. If you couple that with having no real concept of money, as well as no fear of loss, forget about it. You now have a lazy closer who you are wasting appointments on.

Remember, an accountability system is meant to enforce a minimum standard anyone should be able to hit as long as they are putting in the effort. Considering that an accountability system is meant to be a policy, or rather simply a reality within the office environment, it allows management to detach from the negativity and again be the inspiration and positivity that the closer may need in order to get better.

The closer accountability system is very similar to the setter accountability system. There is a minimum standard to hit. If the closer does not hit that in a month, the closer management will sit them down and go through the same process. They will bring up the office standard, show the closer where they finished the month at, and ask them if there's anything they can do to help the closer. Now, on the closer side, considering they are taking daily appointments, generally the problem is not that they aren't working the hours. It's more based on execution. Most of the time, the closers are skipping over the basics and will have to go back to the basics. The closer management will give them the extra training they need to execute the next month. If the closer does not hit the minimum standard next month, they are moved back to being a self-gen. This will require them to knock on their own doors and set up their own appointments to close. They can, of course, move back to being a closer when they start executing correctly again, and we want that. We don't want to move anyone down to being a self-gen permanently. We want to motivate them and help them understand how important it is for them to take care of the leads that are handed to them. Then we want to bring them back as quickly as possible.

The interesting effect of having a closer move down to self-gen isn't entirely that the self-gen will shape up. Actually, a very positive aspect of doing this is that the rest of the closers will take notice and take better care of their leads. This is, in essence, directing the entire department toward the goal. Once the metric is missed once and someone has to move down, the rest of the team will do everything in their power to never miss that metric. No one wants to lose the privilege of being handed leads to run.

While some managers may be afraid to lose a body to run appointments if they have too many appointments to run, remember, an increase in opportunity doesn't equate to an increase in productivity. In fact, the opportunity lost from one person moving down will be offset by twenty other closers working hard with what they have. The production will go up with less opportunity—and that is exactly what we want.

If you focus on opportunity first, again, you are only teaching your team to be average—to take as many appointments as possible and see what sticks. However, if you hold your team accountable and show that execution is the number-one focus of the department, you will have everyone focusing on execution. Once their production is high with low opportunity, give them more.

You will have an incredibly productive team. It's the concept of ironing out the inconsistencies of your team before scaling them. That's the way it should be done.

The fifth aspect of the autonomous system is closer meritocracy. The way we used to have the closer team set up is that there were a few closers at the top who got the most leads. Those closers never changed because they were the "best" closers in the group. They might have been; however, if you hold them there, they get tenure. Tenure will always be accompanied by a lack of perceived opportunity within the office. Therefore, no one else on the closer team will be able to perceive opportunity for moving up. In fact, that will reach all the way down through the self-gen and even the setter department. If a setter can see that there is clear favoritism in the closer department, they either become incentivized to buddy up to management (play the game) or they become disincentivized altogether. Besides, if someone has a position because they are perceived to be the best, a free-flowing meritocracy system based on who is producing the most will keep them consistently at the top anyways. Remember, the purpose of anything we do and any policy we create is to work toward the goal.

The meritocracy system we created is designed to allow closers to earn more opportunities in the coming week based on how productive they were in the week prior. This timeframe is important so that we never have a down week. Basically, at the end of each week, the management team will look over who has closed the most deals while taking into account their close percentage and conditions such as credit turndowns and how many times the homeowners weren't even home to receive the information. Then, at the beginning of each week, we schedule everyone accordingly so that the highest producers from the week before get the most leads while the lowest producers got the least.

Theoretically, this should incentivize everyone to take care of their leads while forcing the lowest producers to put in much more effort. The issue that we run into with our office is that we produce so many appointments that even with a meritocracy system like this in place, we continuously have everyone's schedule filled up. That means that we don't have a meritocracy system at all at times. That is one of the reasons why we promote the top setters, just to offset what the closer team gets so that we can get back to a meritocracy system.

Again, some managers may wonder why we wouldn't want our team's schedule to be filled up entirely. Well, it turns out that the statistics show that if you make a clear distinction between the top producers all the way down to the bottom producers, your whole team will produce more than if there is no distinction at all. It provides motivation based on both fear of loss and the promise of success. It also provides a system that produces money, status, and the perception of opportunity. It has everything. Considering this, we have found it better to have a balance of leads to closer schedule. When you have a couple closers with four leads a day, a few with three, a few with two, and a couple with one, you will see far more production based on who has what motivation. With every form of motivation involved, it's a powerful setup that can't be overlooked. Meritocracy is invaluable within an office setting.

The sixth aspect of the autonomous system is team leads for the closer department. This has quite a different effect than having team leads on the setter side; however, it still hits the three methods of compensation—money, status, and the perception of opportunity. If you take the top few producers on the closer side and make them captains and have them draft their team, you have multiple teams of closers who are looking for the top spot and a win. Competition and camaraderie are great tools to get your team pumped up! While some may think that closers are too professional to take part in a policy like this, anyone will have fun with it for an extra $1,000. That's the money aspect, of course.

As for the status aspect of the team lead position, everyone who's a salesperson wants to separate themselves from the pack. Everyone wants the recognition for being the best. Having a closer lead a team to a victory is rich in status, and they will have a lot of fun with it.

Now as for the perception of opportunity side, this is definitely a little different than on the setter side. Of course, having a status position open up every two weeks allows the rest of the closer team to perceive how they can attain it. That will get them working more. The closer who attains the position really has nowhere further up to go in the company as an employee. The only option they have above that is management, and not everyone wants management. The nifty data that we get from this is that when you see a closer at the top of their game leading a team of people, we can then begin to determine who really has management qualities. If your company is growing and building more offices, the team lead position becomes a fantastic tool to evaluate who has that potential. Often a closer would like to be a manager. Sometimes they may have all the qualities but not any ambition to manage. In that case, we may want to inspire that ambition within them. Sometimes that's not possible. Either way, policies like this are a huge producer of data that we can really learn from.

The seventh and final aspect of the autonomous system is an open management course. I came up with this idea a month into my role as manager. I noticed that every time an office lost a manager, it would take approximately three months for a new manager to be chosen and developed enough to take the position. During that time, production would fall. I figured that if we had a course in place to teach the mechanics and theory of management, we would have people to choose from who are ready at any given moment. That way we don't lose time, opportunity, or production.

Once a week, I now teach a management course that is open to anyone who wants to attend. That is very important. I have seen many offices where the management chooses their top two or three favorite people to develop and only works with them. However, many people don't show management traits because they simply can't perceive the opportunity of going into management. That is exactly what the course is about. Having it be open to everyone gives everyone the perception of opportunity. When you have everyone contributing, you have individuals separating themselves from the pack with innovation and creativity. In fact, a lot of the time creativity will come from people who you didn't even consider as being management material before. That is how powerful perception is.

There are sixty people who work in my office, fifteen of whom regularly attend my management course. That is 25 percent of the office! If 25 percent of the office is motivated by the potential in management, that is an incredibly powerful aspect that needs to be used! I have used this class iron out my own ideas. I have used this class to create new and better incentives while collecting data about what incentives and prizes motivate the team. I have used this class as a focus group for larger seminars. The application of having a team of passionate and interested individuals who are helping build the company is absolutely incredible. As the company expands and more offices open, I can clearly see opportunities for the members of this course. And those opportunities will be easier for them to attain considering they have a much higher understanding of the position, as well as the knowledge of the actual day-to-day functions they need to operate the office. This course has easily become my favorite day of the week.

So, there you have it. The autonomous system is comprised of seven policies that are designed to move all individuals toward the goal through self-direction. That system goes like this:

1. Setter Accountability
2. Setter Team Leads
3. Clear Metrics for Advancement
4. Closer Accountability
5. Closer Meritocracy
6. Closer Team Leads
7. Open Management Course

Using the statistics and data I collected, this system is meant to encompass all aspects of compensation and motivation. If you can create a variation of this structure within your office, you will have successfully created structure that steers the ship toward the goal while simultaneously freeing you up to spend time on other things.

This system is the most recent cog in the machine of creating an empowering office environment. The whole is made up of the sum of its parts, and we want to make sure that we are empowering each part to its fullest potential. Otherwise, the whole suffers.

When the whole is healthy and operating smoothly and productively, you will maintain a self-sustaining office.

About the Author

Matt Wills has a strong background in the sales office environment. After years of being an award-winning top producer for various companies, he currently manages a high-motor canvassing team for Ion Solar. Given the opportunity to build out policies, structures, and culture, Matt played a key role in creating a top canvassing team for Ion Solar that could thrive in any industry.

What makes Matt's methods unique is his departure from the long-standing industry standards. His utilization of data analysis provides great insight into the practicalities of management styles and policies. By understanding the underlying psychology of management concepts, he is able to show where traditional concepts might be short-sighted and can be changed or improved upon.

Matt currently lives in Newport News, Virginia with his wife, Altagracia, and daughter, Michelle.

A free ebook edition is available with the purchase of this book.

To claim your free ebook edition:

1. Visit MorganJamesBOGO.com
2. Sign your name CLEARLY in the space
3. Complete the form and submit a photo of the entire copyright page
4. You or your friend can download the ebook to your preferred device

A **FREE** ebook edition is available for you or a friend with the purchase of this print book.

CLEARLY SIGN YOUR NAME ABOVE

Instructions to claim your free ebook edition:
1. Visit MorganJamesBOGO.com
2. Sign your name CLEARLY in the space above
3. Complete the form and submit a photo of this entire page
4. You or your friend can download the ebook to your preferred device

Print & Digital Together Forever.

Snap a photo

Free ebook

Read anywhere

CPSIA information can be obtained
at www.ICGtesting.com
Printed in the USA
JSHW051720210422
25125JS00001B/8